TALES FROM THE OTHER SIDE OF THE COUCH

INTIMATE TRUE STORIES THROUGH THE LENS
OF A THERAPIST

A YES TO THERAPY COLLECTION

AMANDA CORTEZ   HAKIKAT BAINS

JESSICA LAWRENCE   KEVIN MOODY

MICHELLE MALOTT   WHITNEY WALKER

CORINNA ANNE   TIANA MACK   SARA MCCRAKEN

NICK STAVRIDES   RYAN THOMPSON

MICHELLE JIO   KELLY DUNN

ADRIANA AUCOIN-UNRUHE

GABRIELLE MCQUEEN   LORI YOUNG   JAMES GERI

ISBN: 979-8-9872110-4-5

OH SHIT, I'M A THERAPIST

AMANDA CORTEZ, LMFT

From my childhood backyard, I can vividly remember the view of the sun setting behind the fields of growing broccoli. Sometimes, I felt like I could see forever every time I looked out across that field. As a child, I often climbed into the branches of a small tree that was just my size. I climbed up there for two reasons. One, to avoid my older sister and ensure that she was unable to reach me when it was time to get inside the house for dinner. The second reason was to reflect on my future.

As a little seven-year-old, I was already evaluating and analyzing my life experiences. I was always trying to make sense of people and everything around me, and sitting in the nook of the tree was the best way for me to reflect on my life and ask myself what I may one day become.

"What would I look like?" I would ask myself, "Would I do good things? What kind of job would I have? Would I like who I was?" Funny how such philosophical thoughts never change. I remember only being able to think up to age twenty-five. In retrospect, twenty-five years old was about the age of retirement for a seven-year-old. But while my childhood questions were deep and introspective, I don't think I ever imagined that I would be a therapist.

I remember my first memory of the word "therapist." There was a school-based counselor and everyone knew only the "sad" or "bad" kids went to see her, and they got to play Candyland and eat candy when they did. I constructed an image in my head that I would never get to play Candyland or eat candy because I wasn't bad. But strangely enough, these kids always seemed happy after seeing the counselor and she seemed nice. I just didn't understand, how did they get out of the hard classes to go play games? What was it that this therapist was doing?

It only made sense to me that this therapist had to be someone who could play a matrix over in my mind. I had this belief that this school counselor was some kind of wizard. I thought that she could see my entire life story and future with only eye contact. This led to my intimidation of mental health professionals. If they could get kids out of math class to play games and laugh, what else could they do? Curiosity arose.

Fast forward: I am a Licensed Marriage and Family Therapist, there are no powerful magical tricks up my sleeve, just a person who will actively listen and hold a safe space. I wish the younger version of me knew that: the only magic that was happening in the therapy room was the magic of holding space for another without judgment, with empathy and compassion.

My team and I put this collection of stories together to honor our stories, our journeys to show where we are today, and the incredible resilience we have to withstand and recover quickly from difficult situations and experiences.

Although I had support from friends, family, and my community, there were times I did not know what direction to take, where to go or the best step forward. My journey often became overwhelming and I was forced to learn how to make peace with uncertainty. Anxiety became my best friend, I had to understand it, love it, and honor it, after all, it's a part of me. This deeper understanding of my own inner workings is part of what inspired me to become a therapist. I believe the decision to help others as a therapist is a powerful one, and a story each of us should share.

This is a collection of short stories for comfort, a resting place for your soul, and to know that you are not alone. Putting together thoughts, pieces, and words of encouragement from other therapists, all at different places in their voyage can make this journey feel less isolating. I hope it inspires others in the mental health field to share what is in their heart, step away from judgment and find deeper meaning in their souls, and rest assured others have been there before and they are not alone.

I own a group practice in Silicon Valley and in Santa Cruz, California called "Yes to Therapy." Yes To Therapy consists of a talented group of therapists, who are intelligent, creative, educated, friendly, humble, and skilled. They are culturally informed, compassionate, and most of all, they hold a strong passion for all that they do. When I started my private practice - I craved a resource to let me know how others had felt during their expedition as a therapist, navigating the mental health world. I wanted someone to tell me what to expect on this path, I wanted to hear from other mental health clinicians, I was a sponge, open to absorbing all to come. I wanted to read the words of others who had the same questions and thoughts I did as a therapist.

I asked myself, "Why not create a collaborative, collective of perspectives of those in the mental health field, and what better way to work with my team? This type of resource could be beneficial for those who have been doing clinical work for years or are brand new to the field. After all, every one of us could use a little bit of inspiration!"

I thought I had an idea of what it meant to be a therapist before I even started my master's program. I was the trainee, the "intern", so eager to learn, eager to please, and eager to be the best therapist I could be. Yet, I am still learning what it means to be a therapist every single day.

As I GROW AS A THERAPIST, questions still swirl around in my head, similar to the questions I asked myself hanging from the branches of the tree when I was seven years old, but now with some wisdom of age and purpose attached:

What is the purpose of our lives as therapists?
Can we shut it off when we are not asked to be on the battlegrounds?
Can we find hope after a long day of work?
Are we in this field for the right reasons?
How do I want my community to see me?
How would I like to see my community?
Will I ever finish these daunting hours and see the fruits of my labor?
Could I be a therapist, even if I struggle with anxiety and depression?
Is it normal to love what I do? What is normal anyway?

There were many questions I had as a mental health clinician and no resource filled with stories of those who had gone through similar or not--experiences. As the old saying goes, you should write the book you want to read. So I did just that.

The book you hold in your hands is the book I wish I had access to on my journey navigating life as a new therapist. You will find stories that make you laugh, and some stories that make you cry. It is my hope you find stories that will bring some light and inspiration into your life and your work - no matter what stage of your career you are in.

Being a therapist, like so much of life, is a journey that ebbs and flows. Yes, days will feel long, and sometimes money will feel tight. Some days, you may feel like you are missing the supervision or consultation you need. Other times, you may feel empty, as though no one else understands. There may be doubt, you may undervalue your ability to provide strength in your assessments, your treatment plans, and your clinical perspective.

My wish for you? Remain curious, remain open to learning, and stay present in training, even when it seems difficult to endure. Build bridges in your community, and continue to stay true to your passion.

Even now, there are days I think to myself, "Oh shit, I'm a therapist!" Somedays, I can't even decide what to eat for dinner or I have a long-winded battle just trying to find my car keys, and I am always late! This realization is not just one of immense responsibility. It is also one of deep honor. I have the opportunity to make an impact on another's life. And that is a beautiful thing.

Choosing a healing career was the best decision of my life. Not only do I learn more about myself every day, but I also have much more compassion for the world around me, for humanity, and for myself. I can handle the obstacles that life throws at me with a clear mind and the patience for times when my mind is unclear have accepted that this is okay, too. I cannot guarantee that this road will be easy, but I can guarantee that it will change your life.

1

KYLO

FIRST CONNECTION, FIRST REJECTION, AND DELAYED CLOSURE

HAKIKAT BAINS, LPCC

THEY SAY you always remember your first client. And in my case, it's certainly true. I was in the last year of my graduate program and starting my internship experience in the field. Placed at a school in New York and going into my first day, I recall experiencing every emotion all at once–excited, anxious, proud, scared–you name it! My role at this school was to be a one-on-one therapist for four students throughout the year.

First Connection

In this role, I met my first client–who I will be referring to as "Kylo". Now, "Kylo" is not just any pseudonym (to protect the confidentiality and this client's identity), but it is a name that holds a special meaning and memory for this particular client as you will learn later in the story.

Kylo was eight years old when he was diagnosed with Attention Deficit Hyperactivity Disorder (ADHD), generalized anxiety, sensory sensitivity, and Obsessive-Compulsive Disorder (OCD).

I clearly remember our first introduction. Kylo was hiding underneath his desk at school, sketching on his notepad. I kneeled for us to greet each other at the same level.

"Hi, Kylo. My name is Haki. It's nice to meet you!"

No response.

"I get to work with you this school year in therapy together..."

Eye contact. Still no response.

"I see you like to draw. What is it that you're drawing? Is that from Pokemon?"

"Yeah, it's Charizard. He is a fire Pokemon! See?"

PHEW! My nerves started to settle a bit more as he started sharing more about his drawing. From that first interaction, our rapport started to grow and fade in cycles. There were moments when Kylo would crawl underneath his desk again, and if I came anywhere close to his vicinity, I would be met with screams and airborne pencils. These were the times that made me question my skills, helpfulness, and ability to effectively support my clients in times of need.

In other moments, Kylo would refuse to talk to anyone else but me. He would crawl back to that haven under his desk and pass notes to his teachers stating "Haki," indicating that he was needing my support. These moments felt completely different. In these instances, I found myself feeling gratitude towards Kylo for providing me with this opportunity to support him. I also experienced the pressure to perform well as his therapist, and quite honestly–these were also the moments that helped with my ego and self-assurance.

Our connection and rapport were deep and equally as complex. During outdoor times, we walked to the park holding hands every day. I started coming to school earlier as the year went on because we held a tic-tac-toe tournament each morning before the school bell rang. He named my new plants and school supplies for me; a pencil pouch named "Beth", a pair of shoes named "Mr. Sneaker Boots", and a plant named "Kylo."

We kept a shared secret journal together, where we wrote down our emotions, coping strategies, and new interests to one another, and I felt our connection blossom.

First Rejection

Kylo and I had our moments of building rapport and a supportive therapeutic relationship, but we had equally as many moments when all he wanted was space and distance. However, though these moments included screaming, throwing items, and sometimes even scratches and tears...(many tears), they were always short-lived. Kylo would experience heightened anxiety, become triggered and reactive for about fifteen minutes, and then regulate back to our usual daily routine. Over time, I started to build more of an understanding of Kylo's needs, symptoms, and triggers.

Kylo was the first client I had ever connected with as a therapist. He also turned out to be the first client to reject me as well. We were halfway through the school year, and Kylo did not want to go outside for recess time. Because of this, Kylo and I both stayed back in the classroom as everyone else proceeded to go outside. He crawled back into our usual spot—that cozy space under his desk and he was calm.

As we were sketching together, he said "Haki? I don't want you to be my therapist anymore."

"Oh—okay. Can you tell me more about that?"

"I want a different counselor."

"Thanks for telling me, Kylo. Did something happen? You can tell me if something I have done or said is bothering or upsetting you."

"I don't know."

"Hmm. Maybe we can draw about it? Can you show me how you feel in your drawing?"

I looked at his sketchpad. He was drawing out "NO" in big bubble letters. I proceeded, "Oh, I see. Well, maybe we can talk about it when you're ready? You can request a new therapist, and there's nothing wrong with wanting to do that."

"JUST GO AWAY!"

"Okay, I can give you some space."

I stepped outside of the classroom to give him time. Thoughts started flooding my brain as I waited outside in the hallway.

Perhaps he will feel better in fifteen minutes?

What could I have said or done today that upset him?

I am failing at being a good therapist to Kylo. Should I go back inside?

Is he testing me to see if I will leave him?

Maybe he just needs space and he is overwhelmed by something?

Twenty minutes passed and he still was not ready to talk to me. The classroom came back and he continued his school day. He was calm throughout the day and distanced himself from me. As the hours went on in the day, I began to believe him: he did not want me as his counselor anymore. This did not seem like his usual emotional breakdowns. There was no throwing, screaming, or tears. He was calm and stern, knowing what he needed for himself.

The following day, I approached him to discuss a plan moving forward. We spoke about finding a new counselor, who he was looking for, and how I can assist in the transition. I would be lying if I said I wasn't disheartened and sad to be having this conversation with Kylo. The discussion was calm and professional, as we focused only on our next steps and I was cautious not to bring in any emotions-focused prompts to further trigger him. That evening, I connected with my supervisor regarding this transition.

She told me something during that conversation that I will carry with me throughout my career, "We can't know with certainty what the right next step is for any client. Kylo said this is what he needs at this moment, and that is okay. He may change his mind. He may not. And that is okay."

The next day, when I went back to Kylo's school, he greeted me excitedly and said "Are we having therapy today?"

"Would you like to have therapy today?" I responded.

"Yeah, I changed my mind. I want to do therapy with you and not someone new."

"What made you change your mind?"

"I journaled, and then I talked to my mom and dad last night too. I don't want a new person anymore. Anyways! I don't want to talk about this! Can I show you my drawing?"

We did not speak of his change of heart that day. Each time I tried to redirect us to further explore his experience of journaling and speaking with his parents, Kylo stated that he did not want to talk about it any further than acknowledging that he simply changed his mind. I was relieved, but also confused.

I went back to my supervisor for guidance, who again stated, "Like I said yesterday, it doesn't matter if this is right or wrong, or what made him change his mind as much either. What matters is that this is what Kylo is telling you he needs at the moment. It has changed from before, and that is still okay."

It was certainly reassuring and helpful to hear the calmness in my supervisor's voice. However, I was still left in a place of wonder. I wondered if rejection and reconnection are just a part of therapy. I wondered if I was not digging deep enough. Or perhaps digging too much?

These questions, unfortunately, were left unanswered because Kylo and I both were not expecting our closure to occur in the way it did.

Delayed Closure

The following week started as usual. I was holding sessions with my other clients in the morning and had therapy scheduled with Kylo during the afternoon. I was suddenly called to the administrative office during my lunch break.

"Haki, I am sorry to inform you that there was a COVID outbreak at your grad school. You must grab your stuff and leave campus immediately."

I had heard about the first few COVID cases in New York just the week prior and had not yet realized that this would be a global pandemic lasting for several years. I walked back to the classroom, grabbed my bags, and searched for my students to let them know I had to head out. I could not locate Kylo. Thus, I left a quick sticky note on his desk reading:

"Hi, Kylo! Sorry I had to leave. Let's reschedule therapy when I am back :) -Haki"

Within that same week, things seemed to escalate much quicker than I could have imagined. I moved across the country within just a few days. Within a few months, I started working full-time with children and families at a private practice in California.

Fast forward to the present. Yesterday morning, approximately two years later, I received an email in my mailbox. It was Kylo. He had googled me and found my professional website where I had a "contact me" tab for further inquiries. In this email, Kylo updated me on how well he is doing in school this year, how much more he has learned about Pokemon, and how much he misses our therapy sessions together.

I am now reading this email from my office, with my plant named "Kylo" sitting on my desk. To be quite honest, I don't know how to reply. And given our ethical guidelines in the field, I am not even sure if I am allowed to reply.

Would you?

2

CONNECTION COMES WHEN THE WALLS ARE DOWN

JESSICA LAWRENCE, CSW

POST UNDERGRAD, I was elated to have gotten a counselor position in a large community-based non-profit serving children and families. On my first day, I was warmly welcomed by the director with a framed picture of two otters holding hands, with the capitalized and emboldened word, 'CONNECTEDNESS,' to adorn my desk. It was years later that I would realize how interwoven this theme of *connectedness* would be throughout my work: with clients, colleagues, and within myself.

Pushing into my career, I became aware that a part of my clinical style was to bring my lived experience into the therapy room. This element helped me foster trust and vulnerability in clients and forge meaningful clinical insights. At that time, I was unaware that *connectedness* was often rooted in the "us versus them" mentality, as I considered what made a good clinician and a bad clinician. I often felt like an imposter with my peers, and better aligned and identified with my clients and their stories.

I grew up in an unsafe home and concurrently unsafe community, where hostility, threat, and protection were prevalent themes. This upbringing made me over-align myself with clients and identify with their stories while creating a professional barrier. I was afraid to make mistakes in front of my colleagues and supervisors and this impacted my growth and identity as a clinician greatly: I did not feel effective as a therapist or connected and safe to grow and make mistakes.

While this may seem like a lesson from Psychology 101, finding the right level of *connectedness* was a challenge for me. Oftentimes, I felt too close to the stories of my clients and their families. These were my growing edges as a clinician who has also experienced significant trauma. I found myself passing judgment on my own story, and thinking, "This scenario sounds similar to my own life." Other times, I felt I could not be helpful unless I had personally experienced the challenge my client was going through.

The dichotomy made my head spin. I found myself on a roller coaster of feeling *too* close to some scenarios and too far from others. On one hand, I believed understanding an experience from my own perspective made me a "good therapist." On the other hand, feeling too familiar with a lived experience with a client felt like a barrier to effective therapy.

The balance came from acceptance of my own story and a tremendous amount of self-care. I found that being kinder and gentler with myself like I was with others, allowed me to hold space with them without experiencing the emotions related to their trauma. I began to reject dichotomy and be more open to a spectrum of experiences. Slowly, and gradually, I learned I can support the healing journey without having first-hand experience of the struggle they faced.

The relationship with the clients that I was able to build was not because of sameness, proximity to, or familiarity with their story. Instead, *connectedness* was built on listening. Listening to myself, honoring my own needs. Listening to colleagues without judgment. Recognizing differences of power and privilege, and letting my guard down.

My story doesn't need to be the same as those I help. All I need to be a good therapist is a sliver of trust, a thread of connection, and acceptance of my story, as I help others accept their own.

Clients might say they want a provider that has a story like theirs. They may think "How can you possibly understand my life if you have not experienced what I have?" Sameness helps form a bridge; this is true. Though it is not necessary to do deeply meaningful work.

I have learned that connection is built when walls are down.

It took time for me to learn that important aspects of connectedness are empathy, safety, belonging, and compassion. Empathy for the clients, colleagues, and the extension of compassion for the self. These are building blocks of trust, safety, and belonging, and this is the healing environment that we are appointed to create. I've learned that longevity in this work means creating it for yourself first, before bringing the healing to those you have the opportunity to help.

Many therapists and mental health providers are called to work with the desire to help, often cultivated by experiences in their past. While you support others in finding meaning in their own lives, you may find meaning in yours, too. That's okay. Give yourself the space to be human, to have a past. Let that be validation that the healing work *can be done.*

Below you will find a glimpse into my work. This moment was captured in between sessions in which I wrote some simple words that identified my own lack of self-compassion, and the mental shift that occurred to rewrite my role in the therapy room. By allowing myself the freedom to be human, I find that I am not only more connected to myself, but I also provide my client an opportunity to be more connected to me, a human working to become the best version of themselves possible:

Pick at your inadequacies, stripped clean, to the bone.

Distractions feel good. A veil, shrouding my wounds.

Poke, prod to perfection.

Bend, flex, clean, fresh.

Breathe

Learn, grow, connect.

Breathe

Prepare, organize, plan, and respond.

Breathe

Long, lean, relax your brow.

Breathe

Slim, smooth, tight, too bright.

Breathe

Step light, wet, dry, cool, one bite.

Breathe

Breathe

3

THE UNEXPECTED SOURCE OF TRUE CONNECTION

KEVIN MOODY, LMFT

I was a kid with ADHD. But I was good at hiding it.

While most people saw kids like me struggle in school or friendships, I did not. I had close friends. I was part of the hockey team. I played sports and performed in school and I did such a good job hiding the "different" parts of me, most people would think I was just like them.

Growing up, I learned that connecting with people who were different from me could be dangerous and should be feared or guarded against. This led me to hide my authentic identity and be more on guard with others.

I often felt embarrassed, not because I thought being different was bad, but because I knew that behind warm smiles and friendly greetings and closed doors these individuals were given a stereotypical label they would have to live with for the rest of their life: "That woman is dangerous, that man is lazy," or perhaps, most poignantly, "That kid is so ADHD."

I could connect well. But it came at the cost of hiding my true self. Later, I would learn that the level of connection I was seeking was to be able to show up authentically and still be accepted.

Childhood came to a close, and I grew up and joined the military, certain that this version of shared experience would provide the connection I needed. In the military, we all shared an identity: we lived and breathed our work. We may have come from different places, but our objective was the same. Our haircuts were the same. The way we dressed was the same.

Despite the sameness, I still noticed the subtle lack of connection that I felt in my youth. I still believed that if I should show this world my true, authentic self, I would be labeled "different" and lose any connection I had so carefully curated.

There was a turning point when I entered graduate school and started studying to become a therapist. Grad school and the military had this in common: people came from different backgrounds and from all over the world. However, grad school was the first time I was able to experience connection when expressing different opinions.

In the environment I grew up in, I believed that different perspectives and identities eliminated connection. I learned through passing comments and sideways glances that you can't create relationships with individuals who are different from you. But I encountered a surprise that impacts me to this very day: in a sea of different people and different experiences, I found connection like never before.

I had a grad school professor who remains my mentor to this very day and who had a profound impact on how I view life and connection. He and I were different. Our beliefs varied on everything from social issues to religion, but I found myself learning perhaps the greatest lesson of my life from someone who, at the time, I didn't see eye to eye with. I learned the power of holding space. I learned the power of connection. And most importantly, I learned to see humanity above any labels.

Holding space for someone who experiences life differently than you may be the most impactful lesson I learn in this life. The importance of allowing another individual to live their truth and authentically express themselves, without fully understanding all of the factors that led them to this place has incredible power. Because if we can sit with those who are different from us, and respect them and their experiences, we are on the path to changing the world.

As a therapist, I have learned that nobody has it all together. You don't complete grad school and your clinical hours and miraculously and instantly feel confident and connected. You don't wake up the morning of your graduation without any more lessons to learn, or any more triggers to navigate. Part of being a therapist is facing your insecurities and discomfort - right alongside your client.

I am a therapist who knows the feeling of isolation, and hiding an authentic self - and I can hold space for people who do not have this feeling. I am a therapist with ADHD - and I can hold space for individuals who do not understand what it is like to live in my brain and my body. I am a therapist with values, goals, and responsibilities, and I can listen and support, and respect others who do not hold the same values, goals, and responsibilities.

I believe that human connection is one of the most powerful forces on the planet. It is not found in our similarities, or how well our backgrounds line up. It is not found in the place we were born or the friends we have in common. Human connection is found in having the ability to make space for another, despite the discomfort and despite our differences. It is found in respect - even when I don't identify with another's values or beliefs. It is found in the understanding that we all experience this world differently, and we need more people who acknowledge that this is okay.

I am a good therapist *not* because I have it all together. I am a good therapist because I allow people to show up authentically.

To you wonderful mental health workers - I see your authenticity and respect your work. And my wish for you, more than anything, is that you find a connection in your work, in your home, and in your relationships, with people who model how to hold space for something they may never understand.

4

THE TOO SENSITIVE THERAPIST

MICHELLE MALOTT, LMFT

THE MOMENT that I realized that it was possible for me to be a therapist is a moment I remember clearly. I was in my undergrad psychology class. It was the first quarter after I had transferred to my new university. I had started at this new school after attending community college, and I was still wondering what to major in and had been weighing a few options. Psychology had always piqued my interest. I wanted to know what motivated others to do the things that they do and I wondered if I was capable of making a career out of it.

Growing up, I had been told I was too sensitive. I reacted at times in ways that made others uncomfortable, usually related to a situation that was new and unfamiliar. With a sigh, I would be told to calm down, that it isn't a big deal and I would be left to figure out how to soothe myself from big emotions. I had internalized the reactions of others and worried that I didn't have the capacity to help others. I thought that my reactions were too much as a child, so I figured they were too much as I grew older.

As an adult, I had worked through triggers in therapy and I had a decent grasp on who I was, but sensitivity was still a part of me.

Throughout college, I was told I was still too sensitive to work in the mental health field. But they did not know that my sensitivity could be part of my strength.

I had a college professor during this transformative time in my life who was incredibly endearing. He had white hair and kind eyes and talked passionately about his experience as a therapist. He told the class that he had teared up and even cried with clients before. He talked about how he processed his sensitivities with clients and how it was powerful for them to see that they impacted him.

That was the moment I realized that I could do this work. I realized that my sensitive reactions didn't have to be a problem, as long as boundaries are present and the client isn't made to feel responsible if emotion does come up.

In that psychology class with the white-haired professor, I wondered if I could dare myself to do the hard things, and prove to myself and others that my sensitive personality could make a mark in the mental health field. I wanted to do this, not out of spite but out of the drive to make the work a better place. I declared my psychology major soon after.

After my undergraduate degree, I entered a graduate program that provided a very accepting atmosphere. They taught us to use our countertransference to benefit our clients. For instance, if I begin to feel sad or defensive in session, I was encouraged to sit with that feeling with curiosity. My curiosity would lead me to wonder if my client is feeling the same way I was, if something had been triggered in me to elicit these feelings, or if I am simply reacting to their emotions. Sometimes the answer to that question can be used clinically. Maybe being sensitive wasn't such a bad thing, after all!

Years later as a new therapist, I once again doubted my sensitive nature and I tried on a professional mask. I didn't disclose too much, I listened and tried to hide my emotions. I thought this is what good therapists did! (But, to be honest, I was not very effective.)

Then, I thought back to my own therapy and considered the impactful moments I had encountered while healing. I remembered being a teenager and having a therapist who got angry on my behalf. It was the most validating, impactful moment in therapy that I have had as a client. I felt seen in a way that I desperately needed. Then, I thought of my white-haired professor, crying with his clients because their stories moved him so deeply. His sensitivity validated their feelings and he was a better therapist for it.

With these memories in mind, I asked myself, "Why not let my authentic self, my caring self, shine through?" Remembering the words of my professor paired with the memory of my own therapy, I began to find a rhythm with clients that provides a caring presence and a healing relationship for those I work with while embracing my sensitive and sympathetic nature.

I have come to realize that like others, I used to consider myself too sensitive. I believed I could not hold onto and process my emotions as effectively as others. Once I was able to master the skill of holding space and processing emotions, it made me a better therapist. I can model self-regulation and teach others to do the same. I am not "cured" of being sensitive. But I use it to create intimate and impactful conversations.

I have teared up with clients, just like my professor talked about years ago. If and when that happens I use it as an opportunity to check in with the client, deepen the relationship and be curious about what that brings up for them.

I hope others will dare to do the hard things in life. That they can accept themselves in the messy, sensitive way that is true to them. For the parts that are hard to love, I hope we can show them compassion.

I believe that no one is too much and that as we grow our capacity for acceptance and our authentic selves, we can show more love and acceptance to the world we live in.

5

THE JOURNEY OF AN LMFT
THE TREK FROM GRAD SCHOOL, TO PRIVATE PRACTICE AND BEYOND

WHITNEY WALKER, LMFT

IF YOU ARE on the journey to becoming a therapist, I know you have heard it before: the path to licensure as a therapist is not an easy one. It's a long road with a lot of hurdles (and a LOT of documentation.) I like to describe the journey as a purposeful struggle for your professional progression, one that feels very gratifying and filled with rich experiences. As cliche as it may sound, it may not be easy, but it will be worth it.

Whether you are considering starting the path to becoming a therapist, or are midway through the journey and are curious about what it was like to live through the next step, here is my experience. I know yours will come with its own set of unique challenges and triumphs, but one thing I am confident in is this: this journey will make you a better person, and a better mental health worker. That's something you can count on.

College Graduation

The day I graduated from college at twenty-one, I cried in the bathroom at my graduation dinner. I felt lost and confused about what I was supposed to do with my life now that I was being spat out of my "childhood" and into the adult world. I didn't feel ready to make decisions about who I would be for the rest of my life. But there were a few clues and experiences in college that gave me the nudge into who I may one day become.

Participating in therapy myself in my early twenties was what inspired me to become a therapist. I felt firsthand how it changed my perspective of myself and of things that had happened to me. I yearned to offer the same to others. So, when the tears of college graduation had dried, I began the next step in my journey: graduate school to complete my dream of becoming a therapist.

Graduate School

Completing my grad school degree in psychology left me with a different set of emotions than my undergraduate degree had. The commencement was much more invigorating, I noticed myself excited by everything the speaker was saying. It was then that I realized I had invested my time and money into something I truly cared about, and I was fine-tuning the skills which I knew I would utilize in my profession.

I was confident that with this investment I would be able to do the work that was truly aligned with who I was at my core. Unlike college, I was interested in what I studied during grad school because I knew I would use it, (and I have!) While I felt my confidence gently begin to grow as I left graduate school, something else began to grow: a determination to stick with the goals for my future like never before.

Clinical Hours

This career path allows individuals to explore walks of life that they may never have been exposed to otherwise. And of course, when you have a sense of purpose and direction any load feels lighter. Getting those 3000 hours of clinically supervised work needed to take the clinical exam was overwhelming. It required me to take on difficult roles at organizations where resources were limited and the staff was underpaid and overworked. Yet, it was here I learned that mental health workers weren't doing it for the money, they were there because they believed in the importance of the work.

I met the most amazing people and did some of the most rewarding work of my life during those seemingly endless 3000 hours. It's gratifying when you come into someone's life who is truly troubled and struggling and offer guidance and help when they may otherwise never have received it. Some of the situations I found myself in touched my heart in a way that I will never forget as I could see the light return to the eyes of children and their parents who before had been in great despair. That's what makes this work magical.

Completing my 3000 hours was such a victorious feeling because I knew I'd truly earned it and gained so much incredible experience, insight, and knowledge. Through individual and group supervision, and direct work with clients and their families; I was often pushed out of my comfort zone: the perfect environment for learning. I could feel myself developing my skills and stepping into my role as a therapist like never before. I learned how to work on a team which required pushing through barriers in communication styles and gaining an understanding of what it meant to hold space for others without letting my own emotional experience take precedence.

The Licensure Exam

Preparing for the licensure exam left me incredibly nervous. I felt certain that therapy was my calling and I didn't want this to be the gate that held me back. It's a tough test and took many hours of studying and plenty of practice exams. Passing the exam was a triumph like no other. It was even better than I imagined to cross that threshold and enter the world as a Licensed Therapist.

It sounds silly yet for the first time in my life, I felt *legit!* I was certified to do the work of helping others and earning a living from it. At this point in my career, I watched so many doors and opportunities open for me. There were options to work at clinics, rehab centers, schools, you name it! And I began to realize what I wanted to specialize in and my niche: addiction, eating disorders, and trauma. I couldn't wait to begin my career and watch it develop.

A Licensed Clinician

Since getting licensed 4 years ago, my career as a therapist has blossomed and grown in such beautiful and unexpected ways. My first job as a licensed clinician was at a psychiatry clinic. They assigned me clients of all ages, with a wide range of symptoms and concerns. I learned a lot about what areas I was passionate about and areas I wasn't. I loved how every new client was an incredibly unique exploration into the heart and mind of a fellow human, opening themselves to help and healing.

After I completed my clinical hours and stepped into the role of a licensed clinician, I began to see myself as a professional for the first time. Someone once told me I would never be a true professional or have a successful career due to my reluctance to pick something and stick with it. But here I was, honing my craft and becoming someone who could help others by using my education, work experience, and personal challenges. Two degrees and countless hours later, I was happy to prove them wrong.

Private Practice (and Beyond!)

Two years ago I opened my private practice, something I never thought I would do. I'm living my dream as a business owner, oh the joys of setting your schedule and hours! I'm telling you the possibilities are abundant in this field and the work is transformative. I've cherished every client I've taken on over the years and continue to learn and grow from every one of them. Challenges are present no matter what part of the journey you are on, but I can say with full transparency that these challenges have left me stronger than ever before.

If you've begun, you are on a vibrant path to a rewarding life. It won't look like mine and it will surely come with your own unique set of circumstances. No matter what part of the journey you find yourself on today, the results will surely be worth it. Stay strong, be brave, keep going, and *enjoy the ride!* This life is a beautiful journey and I am so glad you have the opportunity to be on it.

6

HELLO FROM THE OTHER SIDE

A LETTER TO MY YOUNGER SELF, ABOUT THERAPY, RESILIENCE, AND FINDING YOUR VOICE

CORINNA ANNE, LMFT

DEAR 21-YEAR-OLD CORINNA,

Hello from the other side, and *congratufuckinglations* on making it into graduate school! Let me start by saying you have a long road ahead of you. You will laugh and you will cry, and you will contemplate abandoning this dream together and pursuing something less emotionally taxing.

Yet, you will emerge on the other side with a sense of purpose, that I can promise you. You will find your voice and learn to recognize its value in the spaces you insert yourself into.

As you begin graduate school, everything that you know about what it means to be a therapist is going to be challenged. It will destroy your identity as a helper and reconstruct how you perceive yourself in a raw and honest way. You are going to learn how to surrender your own expertise and uplift the expertise of your clients. It's going to be intensely uncomfortable, but this discomfort will fuel your growth.

During this time of building, you are going to question your decision to be a therapist. There will be hard days. You are going to question your abilities and your knowledge because you tend to be hard on yourself. You are going to question why your clients keep returning to your sessions when you believe you have nothing to offer. But you are going to find meaning in the work you are doing, and it is going to fill your soul in ways you never anticipated. And the meaning you discover is going to surprise you.

I am going to be honest with you, you are going to continue to question yourself at 25 just as you did at 21. Don't resist the questions and self-doubt. Rather, hold onto everything you do not know and use it to maintain a sense of humbleness. You do not hold all the answers, nor will you ever hold all the answers. You will adopt the unknown as a strength, not a shortcoming.

This journey is going to teach you more than what you give to people. It will remind you who you are outside of your identity as a therapist. *You will be reminded that you are valuable whether or not you believe you are making measurable changes in your clients' lives.* You will plant seeds in your clients that will grow long after you conclude your relationship with them. You may not see the trees that blossom later on, but find peace in knowing that those seeds are still there.

Good things take time to grow.

You are going to work with challenging cases. You are going to work with clients you don't like. You are going to dread going to a particular session, and you are going to go anyway. You are going to quit jobs and abandon roles due to your own anxieties. But despite this, you are going to find your niche.

I promise that you're going to work with the most beautifully complex people. You will learn to understand the nuance of the human experience. You are going to learn more from them than you can ever learn from books or trainings or classes.

You are going to feel deeply connected to some of your clients. You are going to witness their resilience. You are going to inspire them, and they will inspire you. You are going to bear witness to their best days and their worst days. And you are going to experience unprecedented growth in yourself as you support them in theirs.

There will be times when you are the youngest person in the room. You will question your voice in professional spaces as well as in the therapist's office because of your youth. Sometimes, you will be the only MFT in a room full of doctoral students. You will work with clients twice your age. You will believe yourself to be less than. You will question the knowledge you have to bring to the table. And yet, you will find your voice.

There are lessons you have yet to learn that will impact your whole life. You will learn how to unapologetically take up space. You will learn that you in fact have SO much to say, and others will find value in that. You will learn what it's like to surround yourself with people, professionally and personally, who find your ideas life-changing.

You will burn out. You will lose your ability to empathize at times. But you will learn the true meaning of self-care and embrace it not as a selfish act, but as something that makes you a more well-rounded therapist. Then, you will learn how to set boundaries with yourself and your work.

You will look up to your supervisors, they will become your role models. You will, however, have supervisors that help you discover what you do not appreciate in a leader. Despite all this, they will believe in you and stand behind you in your journey. You will even consider working towards becoming a supervisor yourself.

You will meet the most amazing clinicians and learn from them. You will befriend many of them and they will change your life. They will work their way into your inner circle and provide you with the validation and empathy you so desperately need. They will become your village.

Despite this, you will still feel deeply, deeply alone sometimes. You will look around at your colleagues and wonder what they did to have it all together. Then, you will learn how to embrace your vulnerability and voice it. And you will learn that no one actually knows what the hell they are doing. (You will find comfort in knowing that.)

You are going to find your resilience in yourself and recognize how you have been oppressed. You are going to find grace in knowing that it wasn't you oppressing yourself as you once believed. You are going to forgive your past self and relationships. You are going to heal parts of yourself that you never knew needed healing. You are going to reconnect with your inner child and introduce her to your adult self. Then, you are going to welcome that child with open arms.

You are going to find yourself. You are going to find purpose in what you are doing. You are going to learn how to love who you are and what you have to bring to the table. You are going to surprise yourself with the person you become. Your values are going to change and your priorities will rearrange. You are going to learn to love yourself entirely in the midst of it all.

It's going to be the most challenging time of your life. You will learn to appreciate every part of it.

Good luck, girl! I'll see you on the other side!

With love and gratitude,

25-year-old Corinna

7

A CLINICIAN'S LETTER TO THEIR PRESENT, FUTURE, AND PAST SELF

TIANA M. MACK, PSYD / DR. TMEEZY

DEAR PRESENT SELF,

I am not sure what to tell you. I sense an immense power in you in this exact moment.

I am curious.

In a world of helpers and doers, you are someone special. You see beyond the margins. You know how to pinpoint precisely where you are needed.

It's a gift.

It's a burden.

It's a superpower.

Most of all, it's a response-ability!

You see the seedling and you help it to grow. You are the light in dark, dank places. The warmth of your spirit burns bright and effortlessly. How do you not burn out?

It's as if your spark will never leave you. It has always been with you.

It is the same spark behind your first smile,

Your first cry,

Your first laugh,

Your first sight,

Your first smell,

Your first taste,

Your first touch,

Your first sound,

Your first love.

That spark, which has developed over time, and motivates your decisions to take care. You take care for self, and you take care for co-immunity.

How do you do it?

I see you floating through the pollutions of distress, discomfort, disease, disorder, and disarray.

You are an assessor of the soul. You dig so deep to find water. You bear it all, to rinse it all away.

Where I'm from, we call that dope!

Stay Hustlin', My Friend.

Sincerely,

The Future

DEAR FUTURE SELF,

What does the one that assesses the pain and administers the pleasures want from a world that is known to swallow you whole? Is this the formula to your success?

I have been told that you are often imitated, but never duplicated. You are a healing elixir of mass properties. You got a little bit of this, a little bit of that, a splash of this, a dash of that. You are an *awe-sum* of all of your parts. That is am-azing. You know, "A to Z'ed". No matter where I am, I am wondering where you be.

Where is your beginning, and where is your end? Is it beyond your cracks, your dents, your wounds? Do you ever feel it? Do you even care? You are selfless, and abundant.

Why do you do it? The chaos of it all. The road ahead to you seems clear.

You wiz through the high-ways,

The by-ways,

The free-ways,

The all-ways.

You reach the infinities of the universe. You are an illuminated path. Wherever you go once lasts a lifetime.

Where I'm from, we call that *hope*!

Stay Encouraged My Friend.

Warm Regards,

The Past

DEAR PAST SELF,

My sincerest apologies. I realized that I lied. I hope I did not lie for too long. I am known to take my time, using it as my aid. Time is special to me. It's a creator of parallels and protagonists. Time is a gift. It is a burden. It lets us know how far we have come, even when we have forgotten to look back.

Against time we are defeated. We must quickly learn how to pick ourselves back up. We will always find the strength to keep pressing against time, because we will feel the light, which awakens us, time and time again. Even when it's dim, the light will keep us remembering all that was lost.

The lost love,

The lost safety,

The lost freedom,

The lost opportunity,

The lost joy.

In due time, we will recover our cells. We will nourish every part of our being. We will grow.

We grow into self. We grow into community.

How do I know this? To me, it is clear.

The chaos and revelation of it all.

The defeat,

The despair,

The detachment is a formula of success, support, and surprise. I have seen the water bounce off of your light, reflecting on you, Past, and highlighting an illuminated future. Take that path, the one that is abundant and everlasting. I know you will find ways to navigate the intersections to the best of your abilities.

Where I'm from, we call that cope!

So stay curious. Leap and bound. We are all racing against time.
Keep Shining My Friend.
Without A Doubt,
The Present
P.S. I only hope... to be as dope... as you cope... ya dig!

8

UNDERSTANDING TOLERANCE

AMANDA CORTEZ, LMFT

I HAD on my best pair of professional pants, and a professional top, and my hair was in a loose stylish bun. I sat alone, looking directly at the family of four. I felt my palms start to sweat. Could they know that I was pre-licensed, that the money that they were spending for that session was not for the strong competent therapist, but someone completely new to the field?

I sat posed and polished as could be, with immediate imposter syndrome creeping in. I coached my inner voice to stay positive, "I have trained for this, I spent years in graduate school, I am halfway into my 3000 hours, and I have had excellent supervisors and compassionate role models who have helped me understand what it means to be a therapist. I deserve to be here and to help these people."

"Besides," I told myself, "I am in debt and close to only making minimum wage for this hour with this family. I am basically paying to be here."

I calmed my thoughts and reassured myself that I was capable and ready for anything that my role as a therapist would present to me.

I considered the fact that I wanted to be an original therapist, with all my own ideas, all while maintaining the traditional modules and interventions. I didn't want to be like every other therapist. I wanted to add my own style.

While these thoughts filled my mind the first day, little did I know what my future as a new therapist would hold, or the challenges I would encounter that would make me a stronger, more impactful mental health worker today. "Original" didn't even begin to scratch the service of the experience I would soon have.

I bonded well with my supervisor, who I will call "Tolerance" for the sake of the story, not only because she had such patience for me as a new associate, a term once referred to as "intern," but also due to the struggles my supervisor faced. Tolerance taught me the value of being a supervisor. As her intern, I felt special, I felt heard, but I was just getting my feet wet in private practice and this new role was a big learning experience for me. I was quiet and reserved, I was timid and overworked. But I was eager.

She was a compassionate therapist, she provided time and room for those who came to her. I knew her clients loved her and felt at home and supported in her presence. I knew because we often worked with the same families: I worked with the kiddos and she worked with the parents, the mothers, and everyone else in between.

This is how I thought of Tolerance: a compassionate, well-adjusted therapist with so much to teach me.

But soon, everything would change.

After almost two years of having her as a supervisor, I was feeling more confident than ever. I was ready to grow, ready to immerse myself in a business plan with her, to merge ideas. Yet, there was a distance that grew between us, she was no longer the career-oriented supervisor that I remember. Instead, she seemed as though she was wrapped up in a misery none of us could quite pinpoint.

At first, the warning signs were small, like smelling the scent of cigarette smoke while sitting in the waiting room when I was the first to get into the office. It was an unusual scent that I had not smelled in the office before. Furniture began to break and remained un-fixed. Doors would remain unlocked from days prior, alarms not set, keys missing, along with unpaid balances for weeks at a time.

Tolerance remained as present as she could be in sessions until she couldn't. I took the brunt of many of her mishaps and so many times wished that I wasn't the recipient of the frustration from clients and other administrative members running the office. I remember dismissing my own thoughts and feelings around the dynamic because I wasn't exactly sure what was going on. There is no class in grad school about what to do when your supervisor starts acting unprofessional! This was uncharted territory.

Tolerance began to look disheveled, to wear the same outfit days in a row and not the typical jeans that we know we could wear every day if we could. These were the same white pair of pants and the same bright-colored top. It was apparent that she was struggling and should have stopped seeing the clients she cared about and the work that she loved. It was clear that something was going on in her personal life, and she wasn't managing well. But what does one say when this is your supervisor? Where does an associate draw a line in a dynamic in which the other has the power? It was my professional career in line, I thought I had to "suck it up and do the job in front of me."

It wasn't until we were sitting in group supervision that I noticed bruises all over her arm. She was petite, the bruises were quite large. I distinctly remember glancing at her bruises, then making eye contact with Tolerance. I looked back at her arm and looked away. I tried my best to not make it obvious that I caught a glimpse of what might be happening in her personal life. I could see that she became uncomfortable, she pulled down her sweater to cover up in a guarded way. I will never forget that moment in time. No one said a thing, how could I be the only one to notice? I was not particularly close to anyone at the practice, I kept it to myself.

Thoughts, miles a minute were shooting through my head-- should I say something? Should I pull her aside to check in? Was she okay? Could she hear my thoughts? I left group supervision that day full of questions, fears, uncertainty, and sadness.

Have you ever seen someone in so much pain that you wonder if they even realize that they are still alive? Someone who wears their pain on their sleeve, but you wouldn't dare ask because you didn't know them well enough to probe? My kind supervisor and compassionate mentor became a person filled with that kind of pain. Her grief, anger, and everything else she kept hidden seemed to overtake Tolerance.

Then, she became mean, I knew it wasn't her authentic self. She would laugh at my mistakes, she would gently push my feelings aside. As time went on, she became more tired and irritable, nothing like the Tolerance I once knew.

One afternoon before clients, I took her aside and checked in about some odd behaviors I had noticed. Being able to do that as an associate was very empowering, though I was distraught at the same time by having to confront my mentor. I never thought I would be in that situation as a therapist, but there it was, happening all in front of me and at me all at the same time: my supervisor was clearly unwell. And I didn't know how to help her.

I felt guilt, I felt frustration, and my emotions were complex. It was challenging to know that I would have to come up with a Plan B if she continued to live her life this way. How could I continue to see my clients while under the care of her license if she was struggling? I called

CAMFT, (California Association of Marriage and Family Therapists) to see what they advised. As I was dialing out the letters, I felt a mild level of relief but an uprise in blame. Here I was, calling CAMFT about my supervisor? I felt uneasy and uncomfortable, but I had already confronted her and did not see a change.

Making this call felt like I was calling the cops, as though the lawyer on the other line would know exactly who she was and immediately revoke her license and put her in jail. Which, now that I look back, may have been better than what was about to happen. Unfortunately, there was no relief from that call, and I was only left with more confusion. No immediate action was taken to fix this situation and I was left more frustrated than before.

I began to check in with her multiple times a week to make sure she was okay until one day. I would call when I could, or check in face to face when I could. Until one day, I received news that Tolerance was in a coma at the ICU on life support. This is how Tolerance left this world.

My wonderful mentor and inspiring leader had her life taken by addiction before we even knew what was happening. Tolerance hid that pain until she couldn't anymore. Not only had I lost a colleague and supervisor, but I also lost a friend. And it would be my job to pick up the pieces and manage the grief her passing left behind.

I chose not to go to her funeral, potentially seeing clients and making sense of the emotions that were to come from it was not something that I had room for at the time. (Harsh, I know, but part of being a therapist is knowing your boundaries.) I was trying to save emotional space for clients in making sense of the loss. As weeks went on, I would make room for the parents of children whom I worked with to grieve. I continued to push my own level of tolerance, and my bandwidth for how to clinically navigate through this.

I did everything I was supposed to do, that Tolerance had taught me to be, and still, the questions swirled in my head, "How do you explain to clients that their former therapist was no longer alive? How do you even begin to process this with a client if you are both grieving over the same individual? How do you even begin to offer the client another therapist after the abrupt sudden loss?"

The questions were complex, not to mention, the immense guilt of not being able to help.

I know that I can't be the only therapist that has had to experience this while having a supervisor. I heard stories like this in graduate school, about how to make sure you always have your hours signed because "you could instantly lose your supervisor along with all your hours."

It seems such a bitter way to view a human life: a signature on a page showing hours was complete. You never think this could happen to you, but the likelihood of it happening, probably won't," version of the story. Like a scare tactic that is put on those in graduate school to create an even more anxious environment than we might already be in.

But it can.

Fast forward to today; my own private practice was initially a passion project, not only a way to work through my own grief, because of my experience with Tolerance, but because I had always dreamt about bringing to life this passion of mine. I truly did not realize how many amazing therapists would want to work at the group practice. It is incredible how therapists bring their unique style, spirit, and creativity to Yes To Therapy.

My mind shifts back to the time in the office with my professional pants, loosely curated stylish bun, and nervous heart. I thought of the imposter syndrome that threatened to enter at any moment, and how I was focused on saying just the right thing, at just the right time. I thought of how I would connect with Tolerance after the session, how she would guide me gently through hurdles and show me a first-hand example of empathy. And I thought of how far I had come since that day, and the situations I had been forced to endure.

I think of my practice now, and the associates that have worked with me, how I have worked to be the example of embodied love and understanding. I think of how nervous they seem, and how despite how well you can prepare, some things in life catch you off guard, knock the wind out of you, and force you to fend for yourself. It's times like these that we are reminded of our own resiliency and strength.

And then, I think back to my mentor and the pain she kept locked inside. I thought of the grief she wore on her sleeve and how I have grown since the day I received that phone call that she was gone. I reflect on how I was forced to decide how to best be a light in the world during the dark time.

I thought of how I have grown.

I thought of how I have changed.

I thought of Tolerance.

Some days it is hard to believe that it has been several years since Tolerance left us, and many years since I started Yes To Therapy. It is during moments of this deep reflection that I am reminded of my career as a therapist and the resilience of human nature.

The world still needed Tolerance. We never had enough.

But her memory lives on in this: a reminder to my clients, my loved ones, and the world that you are strong and brave beyond measure. And that is enough.

9

IT COULD NEVER HAPPEN TO ME: EXPERIENCING THE SUICIDE OF A CLIENT AS A LICENSED THERAPIST

SARA MCCRACKEN, LMFT

SUICIDE. Suicidal Ideation. Self-Harm. These are all concepts you become familiar with pretty quickly when training to be a therapist. I was already working with kids that were engaging in self-harm and was having to assess for suicide by the time these concepts were brought up in grad school. While a daily part of my training, I never thought these things I learned about would lead to an actual suicide.

I remember the day I first learned about suicide in grad school. The professor that was presenting had a client who was successful in his attempt and was sharing his experience as a mental health worker navigating this crisis. I remember the way he portrayed his experience, while heartbreaking, came off as more of a warning. He told us that a client's suicide could happen, but it was rare. I remember thinking during that lecture, "That would never happen to me."

That was in 2019. In 2021, it did.

I was working as a therapist towards licensure. It was my first job after practicum, and I had the title of Primary Therapist. I was stoked. I felt like I had finally made it and was progressing in my career. I was working with eating disorders and many of the clients I saw had suicidal ideation or were actively engaging in self-harm. At the time, I didn't realize how close the reality of suicide was to those I was working with. Eating disorders have one of the highest mortality rates so in my eyes, suicide wasn't the main concern, the eating disorder with its plethora of health complications was.

When I was assigned to the client that would ultimately pass, seeing that he had attempted in the past didn't scare me. At this point, suicide was a topic I was familiar with. I knew how to assess for it, how to get parents involved without the client feeling like confidentiality had been broken, and when to know that a higher level of care was needed. In fact, the whole time he was in my care I met with him and did a suicide assessment daily, and worked very closely with his parents.

After three months of work, he had made great progress and was getting ready to discharge from the program within the next couple of weeks. He appeared happier, lighter, and had future goals. The eating disorder had significantly reduced and he was no longer having suicidal ideation and self-harm urges. I remember the last morning I saw him we did a group check-in and for the first time, he checked in as happy.

Then, everything changed.

I remember coming in to work that morning. It was a beautiful April day. I remember being told that his mom had called, and wanted me to call her back. I figured it was due to him not wanting to come into the program that day, which was not unusual, so I didn't rush to call her back right away. When I finally did call, the voice on the other side of the line said he had hung himself the night before.

Very clear and simple words, yet I didn't hear them. I remember the meaning of the words not sinking in and I remember saying "I'm sorry, what?" So, she repeated herself. She gave me some more details and hung up.

You never know how you are going to handle a situation until you are in it. I wish I could convey what I felt after hearing the news, but no words could do it justice. I remember being in disbelief, in shock, and feeling overwhelmed. I know I started crying at some point and was eventually sent home. Everything else is pretty much a blur.

It is uncharted territory dealing with the loss of a client. As therapists, we are well-versed in client confidentiality, we can't disclose information about a client, even when it is impacting us greatly. Because of this, I couldn't talk about the situation with anyone, and that in itself put me in a dark place. I was left feeling like I had to deal with this alone and was unable to reach out for support.

In the aftermath, I was questioning every step I had taken with this client. I was questioning everything I had said. I told myself, "You should have seen the warning signs, that was your job." This led to guilt, shame, and sadness. I was in a field designed to help people and I had failed in the worst possible way. For a long time, I held the belief that his death was my fault. If I had just said or done something different, he would still be here.

The shame I felt was further exacerbated by the environment I was working in at the time. Upper management felt that I should be ready to return to work after two days. When I felt differently, they questioned why it was taking me so long to move on, this in turn made me question myself, as well. "Work says I should be over it and ready to return so why aren't I?" my internal voice said over and over. "I only worked with this client for three months, is my sadness valid?"

The feelings of guilt and blame I was harboring came back with a vengeance when I was put under investigation. The company wanted to make sure I wasn't at fault and had done everything correctly.

While I understood this was protocol it put me once again back in the cycle of grief and questioning, leaving the intense emotions to start all over again.

I learned in doing my own research that having a client commit suicide happens to a lot of us, and it is rarely discussed, leaving individuals like myself to grieve in silence. The following statistics I wanted to share here so others, like you, are prepared and not left in the dark. One caveat to these statistics is that they were published in 2017, meaning they have most likely changed in the last six years, and new data has yet to become available:

- 1 in 7 therapists reports losing a person in therapy to suicide.
- 1 in 3 clinical graduate students will work with an individual who attempts suicide at some point during their training,
- 1 in 6 will experience death by suicide of an individual they are working with
- 1 in 6 individuals dies by suicide while in active treatment with a healthcare provider.
- Working with people who are at high risk for suicide is considered the most stressful of all therapy practice endeavors.
- Therapists who lose a person to suicide may experience such a loss to the extent that they would experience the death of a family member.
- The loss of a person in therapy by suicide can become a career-ending event, if not handled correctly.
- The distress therapists experience after losing a person in treatment to suicide can be further exacerbated by possible legal actions. Of those who die by suicide, 25% of family members choose to take legal action against the individual's mental health care team (Bongar, 2002; Kleespies, 2017).

Going through that experience as an associate, while difficult, was a blessing in disguise. It made me stronger, it made me more aware and prepared for the future. It also made me step back and evaluate the career I was in and ask myself if ultimately this career was going to be too much for me. I also learned that the training I received up until this point in no way prepared me for this event. I think I would have felt more prepared if I had known more of the statistics like the ones I shared above.

As I stated previously, in grad school client suicide was discussed as a rarity. As if it is something that happens infrequently. I think if I had learned that it was more common than I was led to believe, I would have been more prepared. It would have been in the back of my mind, allowing me to be not as shocked when it occurred.

The death of my client broke my heart and it is something I am still dealing with to this day. I know in sharing my story, I can help others feel less alone if this happens to them. For those of you who also go through this experience, my heart aches for you. Know that while we may not talk about it, as much as we should, many of us have gone through a similar experience. Remember, there is no right or wrong way to grieve the loss of a client. Making sure to take care of yourself in whatever way feels right is key. Unfortunately, suicide is a devastating reality of the work we do. While I've found that currently there is a lack of resources for therapists, I know that with more awareness this can change. We don't overcome tragedy by leaving it in the shadows. Instead, we find resolution and healing by bringing our challenges into the light.

123

1. Bongar, B. (2002). *The suicidal patient: Clinical and legal standards of care.* Washington, DC: American Psychological Association.
2. Kleespies, P. M. (2017). *The Oxford Handbook of behavioral emergencies and Crises.* New York: Oxford University Press.

3. Meichenbaum, D. (2017, September 28). *For Therapists: Coping with the Suicide of a Person in Therapy*. Good Therapy. https://www.goodtherapy.org/blog/for-therapists-coping-with-suicide-of-person-in-therapy-0928175.

10

THE DARK ROOM

NICK STAVRIDES, CADC-I

MOST PHOTOGRAPHERS ARE familiar with a "Dark Room." This is a room from which normal light is excluded and used for developing photographs. Sometimes, as I reflect back on my childhood home, the vision that comes to mind is a Dark Room, although there weren't any photographers in my family. Instead, the Dark Room in my house growing up was due to my mother's lifelong battle with addiction and illness. The Dark Room was a place where the shades were drawn, the lights were off, and were it not for the moans and screams, one might think the room was empty. But I knew there was a deep level of sadness and hurt that lived in that room that would follow me through adulthood.

Despite the Dark Room, my early childhood was quite normal: full of sports, video games, homework, TV, books, and everything else a child of the 80s might experience. Young MC and Aerosmith would blast on my Walkman and life seemed normal and happy. As my childhood rolled into my teenage years, Young MC and Aerosmith tapes became Soundgarden and Pearl Jam CDs. Video games and sports became girlfriends and parties and still, life was normal and happy.

But amid this normalcy, there was an underlying secret; a painful, heavy, burdensome shame and guilt that existed deep inside me, despite how normal life seemed to those looking in. But this was not part of life I wanted to showcase to the world. So, I learned to conceal and hide my pain through silence and compliance.

I did not discuss the Dark Room with anyone, though no one explicitly told me to keep quiet. Sharing this secret would have made it more real. I believed that in talking about the Dark Room and my mother inside, the reaction of others would force me to face a reality I was unequipped emotionally to confront.

"This must be how every family lives," I would force myself to think. "Every family must have a Dark Room to keep their mother safe." This denial kept me able to blissfully engage in life outside the Dark Room.

Despite the attempt to keep myself sheltered, I could not deny that the Dark Room had a profound impact on me, even in early childhood.

As a young child, my father would tell me daily that "Mom is sick, please check on her." I was happy at the thought of seeing my mother, I loved my mother. But then heartbreak would ensue: the constant letdown of a mother who was always sleeping or too sick to engage. This was a pattern of constant disappointment.

I gritted my teeth through the disappointment and made up my mind to be the best son in the world and step into that dark place. I would get my Mom water when she was thirsty, empty her throw-up bowl, count out her pills, and put them in the right order so she wouldn't miss one. Surely, everyone must clean out their mom's kidney-shaped "throw-up bowls" now and then. I was convinced that this was a normal part of life.

As my teenage years approached, the Dark Room felt heavier and my mom's sickness grew deeper. The room felt more like a black hole sucking the energy and life clean out of my body. In it, time stood still, frozen in fear and sadness.

At age 15, I discovered alcohol was the perfect remedy for all of my issues, and with enough of it, I could overcome the shame that seeped inside. It was a magical potion that took away the pain, provided social status, established connection, afforded sexual intimacy, and most importantly, was an escape. Or so I believed.

I was also able to balance out some of the dysfunction at home with a talent for playing baseball that I'd fostered from the age of eight. I was a pitcher, and the mound was a place where I had complete control. On it, I was overpowering, successful, validated, and feared by those that faced me. At age 18 however, I tore my rotator cuff and never pitched again. Devastated, my after school activities in the Spring of my senior year turned to drinking almost daily.

At home, my mother's screams grew louder and her condition grew even more terrifying. As I'd look upon her fragile body in the same bathrobe for days, my heart would clench. Every cell in my body wanted me to run away, but guilt and fear kept my feet planted beside her. Checking on her no longer meant fetching water, but rather tasks like picking her naked body off the bathroom floor and getting her back to bed. Her eyes often rolled into the back of her head, her body soft and yet rigid at the same time. This is what the Dark Room meant to me.

After graduating college and moving into my first apartment in New York City, my journey into adult life began. Over the next 20 years, I got married, had kids, and held a job, just as I was expected to do. During this time, I visited my mother on occasion, she was on oxygen at this point and able to move about the house but rarely left. My parents moved into a different home, but the Dark Room stayed the same. There was a beautiful backyard with lots of sunlight but the shades remained closed nonetheless. My mother would walk out of the bedroom to hug my kids and they would sometimes lie on the bed with her. But the visits were short as they ended when she needed to rest.

Though I may have seemed to have my life together from an outsider's perspective, the turmoil and uncertainty of my childhood continued to seep into aspects of my adult life. I regularly drank, did drugs, acted out, and behaved erratically. It was as if I spent my life metaphorically both in and out of the Dark Room: at one moment it seemed that I was living a life filled with normalcy and understanding, and in the next moment, I was covered by darkness and unable to see my way out.

I was desperate for a normal life, and so I did all I could to have one. I chose a job in finance because I was good at math and it paid the bills. I maintained friendships by using wit, sarcasm, and my sense of humor. And I used the judgment of others as a way to cope with my deep sense of insecurity. My job, my personality, my marriage, and parenthood all shielded others from seeing anything that lurked below the surface level of my life. But, much like my younger self, I was unable to escape the existence of two separate lives: the one the outside world perceived and the Dark Room inside of me.

In February 2019, the parts of myself that continued to deny the existence of the other finally caught up to me. I woke up in a hospital bed (thankfully not handcuffed to it) after passing out in a parking lot just feet from my car due to intoxication. This would mark the beginning of a recovery journey that found me going back into my Mother's bedroom to face my greatest fear: A dying mother and feelings of abandonment, loneliness, and despair.

I'd been seeing my therapist, who I'll call David, for two years before the session which changed my life. I forget exactly how it began, but I was explaining to him that I felt stuck. After exploring the feeling further, I identified fear as the root of it. "It's like I'm standing in my Mom's bedroom!" I exclaimed to him.

At this point, he suggested that I close my eyes. He asked me the age where this fear presents strongest.

"I'm nine," I replied.

He allowed me a moment to connect to that age. My feet were flat on the floor, hands on my thighs and this is when I began to close my eyes. I allowed myself to be transported to the place of my childhood.

"Where are you?" he asked.

"I'm outside my Mom's room and I don't want to go in."

David then asked me why I didn't want to go in the room. I remember telling him that I was terrified and worried.

"I think my Mom's going to die," I told him.

David then asked me what I needed.

"I need to feel safe," I answered.

"How will you feel safe?" David asked.

My answer was, "I don't want to be alone."

"Invite someone into the room," David instructed

At this point, I imagined my current self standing beside 9-year-old me outside the bedroom door.

"Hold his hand," David suggested to my grown self.

My eyes were tightly shut, and I imagined the hallway that led to the Dark Room. I saw my 9-year-old self with his blond bowl-shaped haircut, socks pulled to his knees and frightened blue eyes looking up at me. I could feel his little hand in mine, supple and fragile. I gripped it tight, but gently.

"Are you ready to go in?" I asked my younger self.

"Not yet," my 9-year-old self replied.

"What do you need?" I asked.

"For you to come with me," he said.

We both opened the door and walked slowly into the Dark Room. We approached my mother who was sleeping and we sat together at the end of the bed. Tears began streaming down my face as I sat on David's couch, while my mind was at this place of fear inside my mother's bedroom. My tears were hot and salty and I could feel them pooling at my mouth and dripping down to my chin. My chest heaved as I gasped for air, half allowing my tears, half choking them back.

These tears were a symbiotic healing where I unleashed decades of repressed sorrow as an adult. It was at this moment that my 9-year-old self was able to express his feelings and be supported in them, rather than stay stuck and frozen in repressed sadness and terror. Both of us were finally able to be seen by one another. I had become my own self-loving parent.

I was encouraged by David to allow these feelings to fully come through me and stay with the experience. The tears fell faster, and my face felt flushed and wet. After a minute or two, I felt a rare sense of relief. I arched my head back taking a deep breath, my eyes still tightly shut.

I was now hugging my 9-year-old self on my Mother's bed and repeatedly telling him, "You're safe. I'm here. You're safe, I'm here."

My mother died of cancer in May of 2020, two years before I returned to her bedside in a therapy session. My session with David was one of the most significant moments in my healing journey. Before the session, I was unable to properly grieve and accept her death. First, I needed to grieve the loss of parts of my childhood.

From there, I was able to focus on my mother, empathize with her life of pain and struggle, and finally forgive.

This experience has been a major contributor to my devotion to helping others who also struggle with trauma. I am grateful for the gifts of therapy, sobriety, and the people with whom I'm surrounded doing similar work. Our power, ability to grow and the impact it can have on all those that we touch along the way meets me today with a newfound gratitude for my mother.

A "Dark Room" is defined as a room with no light or with a safelight for developing light-sensitive photographic materials.

Re-parenting my inner child and guiding him back through the dark led us both to a safelight. No longer tethered to stuck, unchanged images and memories, I can develop new healthy thoughts and aspirations: free to change, adapt, grow, and move forward, out of the Dark Room.

11

GIFTS FROM THE STORM

AMANDA CORTEZ, LMFT

WHEN I WAS six years old, I was attacked by a dog. I was living on a small farm with my family during this time, and access to mental health services looked different than it does today. My mother, worried about the potential for me to never want to be around animals again, found a therapist who would come to our home. At this time, in 1994-1995, you could get a home visit from a licensed therapist for a grand amount of $90.00 for a 60-minute session. And so, the appointments were scheduled.

I remember this man quite well; he was a good therapist, at least he seemed that way to a child like me. He looked like me and my family and he regularly praised me for the artwork that I was so proud of. These things were important to a child like me and allowed me to feel comfortable and seen.

From what I can remember, I never said a word to this kind man who came to visit after the dog attack, but I sure liked to draw pictures of my family and show them off. He had a calming presence and I felt safe when he was around. Occasionally, I was even grateful the attack had allowed me to meet the quiet man who came to our small farm once per week.

But he wasn't around long. When he suggested other members of my family get involved in therapy, my father determined these house calls had gone on long enough. In my father's eyes, not a man in the world was going to come into our home and tell us how to be a family. I cried and gave my therapist my best ninja turtle shirt as my way of saying thank you during our last session. It's funny how someone you don't even remember speaking with can leave such a lasting impression on your life.

My first therapist impacted me in profound ways. He had taken the scariest moment I had experienced in my short six-year-old life and turned it into a gift. Instead of associating the dog attack with something terrifying to reflect on, I now remember it as an opportunity to connect with a kind person in new ways, a person who truly saw me and could communicate in the ways I was most comfortable. It was as if the dog attack had been a storm and his presence had been a brief but welcome gift at the conclusion. Little did I know that my future consisted of helping others find gifts amid their own storm, just as he had done for me.

As a therapist, my goal is to always connect with my highest good. There are days when being a healer is draining and days when I feel like I have made the biggest difference in the world. But what keeps me bringing it back, time after time is the knowledge that so many people need to be reminded of that there is a light at the end of the tunnel, or a rainbow when the clouds finally clear. There are gifts at the end of the storm. Some of these gifts look like a deeper understanding of yourself. And some of these gifts look like a therapist providing a safe space to communicate the way you feel most comfortable. My highest good is helping others acknowledge those gifts and embrace them fully.

What I do is a fundamental part of who I believe I am today. As a therapist, we learn to look pain right in the eye. We learn what it feels like to sit with another person's uncomfortable muck, and their pain, and sort through it. To put it simply, we sit with clients in the middle of their storm.

In my earlier years in becoming a therapist, I was passionate about wanting to help others but was still unburdening the parts of me that were captivated by forces of accomplishment and over-achievement. In my early career, I know I was still recovering from my own storm, and that manifested by operating from a "fix-it" focused lens, rather than a "sit with it," perspective. I wanted to fix my client, and I wanted to fix them now! But even in that, there was a lesson. What I learned is this: if you are fixated on your own storm, there is no way you can help clients out of theirs.

Whether you are a therapist or the average person on the street, the same fundamental truth remains: if we can withstand the high wind and rains, and can stay present when the temperature drops and the clouds roll in, well that is when the gifts appear. It is only then can we find the beauty, self-acceptance, and authenticity of what we cannot change. It is only then can we begin to truly appreciate who we were created to be.

Therapy and becoming a therapist is about the ability to sit in darkness, to be present when it's uncomfortable, and to know that the light will come again, and the overwhelming feelings will become tolerable if only we can wait. And we may just end up stronger for it.

For those of you who are thinking of entering the field, are currently in graduate school, have already graduated, are licensed, or are in transition, always remember your value and your worth. Set healthy and clear boundaries, ask for that raise, read books, listen to podcasts, and tap into your creative part. The endless hours of burning through eucalyptus candles, sage, and palo santo could not have taught me how to do that. It took patience, growth, and time. The hard days and seemingly overwhelming challenges may at times make you feel like giving up. But it is during those times you remember the gifts that are awaiting you when the rain clouds clear.

When in the field after grad school, you become a stronger clinician, you begin to give yourself more credit for your work, long days begin to get even shorter and the work becomes much more natural because perhaps we start to believe in ourselves more. You don't have to know everything, there is room for error, and you are always learning. Remain curious, find the inner calm, embrace all of who you are, and fall in love with yourself, even the parts you don't like.

And now, a few gifts for you, my fellow mental health worker. These breathing/somatic and grounding exercises were written by **Gabrielle Gabai**, a fellow LMFT, and were intended to help you create peace, grounding, and understanding during the challenging times you will face in your career. These are items that I have used extensively when the daily responsibilities of this field felt too great to handle. They are, in the most literal sense, gifts from the storm. May they bring you peace and a feeling of lightness when the rain clouds roll in, and remind you that even dark days come with a silver lining.

Breathing/Somatic Exercise

Let's take a few moments to focus on your body and breath.

Start by noticing how your breath feels right now in its natural state. Notice how deep or shallow your breath feels. Take note of where in your body you feel your breath the most (Your throat? Your nasal passages? Your chest?) Become aware of if your breath is filling your belly or your chest. Notice if your breath begins to change now that you have begun to focus on it.

Now, begin to gradually deepen your breath. Allow your belly to rise with each inhale, filling with air, and feel your belly fall with each exhale, allowing all the air to escape from your lungs. Focus on expanding your breath until it comes to a comfortable, deepened state.

Continue with this breath as you start to tune into your body. Gently scan through, taking note of how your overall body state feels at this moment. Begin noticing any areas that are calling for your attention. These areas may feel tight, tense, or in pain; maybe these areas feel open and spacious. Use your intuition, without judgment, to just notice any parts of your body that desire your attention.

In a moment, you will close your eyes or bring your gaze gently down. Once you do this, you will begin to visualize your breath being sent to these areas of your body that need special attention. If you have more than one area that is calling for your attention, you will send breaths to each part, one by one.

With each inhale, imagine the breath coming through your body directly into this desired area.

With each exhale, you allow the breath to flow outside of you, carrying with it any tension or sensation that was arising.

You will continue sending these breaths to your body for as long as it feels intuitively right. When you are ready to stop, take three more deep breaths, filling your entire body with air and releasing.

After those breaths, take a moment to tune back into your body. Notice how you feel. Become aware of any changes in your mind or body. Take note of any areas that still need your attention. Notice without judgment. Send compassion to yourself.

Now close your eyes, and breathe...

Grounding Exercise

Let's use this moment to practice grounding.

Start by taking three long, deep breaths.

Now, begin to notice the ways in which your body has contact with the world around you.

Start with your feet. Notice where they are in relation to your body, as well as how or if they are making contact with objects around you. What does it feel like for your feet to be making contact, or not making contact, with the ground, chair, etc?

Next, begin scanning any other areas of your body that are touching the world around you. Observe parts of your body that may be touching your body itself. Notice how your body feels as it makes contact. Grow awareness of the textures of what you are touching. Notice the temperature of the object(s). Become curious, as if it's the first time you have ever felt this sensation.

Now notice the parts of your body that are not making contact with anything. How does that feel?

Tune in, and ask your body if it needs any adjustments. Do you need to change positions? Do you need to stretch? Does your body need more grounding and contact with the Earth? Do you need more space to expand?

Take a few moments to intuitively move your body. Trust the way in which your body needs to move, and try not to hold any judgments. Move freely.

After you've given yourself the space to move, find your resting space once again. Close your eyes, and take three more deep breaths.

You've made it.

12

HEAVY METAL, WHOLE-ASS HUMANS, AND HONORING THE AUTHENTIC SELF

RYAN THOMPSON, LCSW

LOOKING at the course syllabus online and realizing my academic journey was fast approaching its harrowing conclusion, a sense of wistful dread began to come over me. It took some time to realize that feeling was the abyss of a career firmly staring back at me. Perhaps it was always there waiting for me or perhaps it was the byproduct of a conjuring that took place over seven years of higher education and all the inherent pits and valleys.

Regardless of the origin, one thing was certain: after having a defined course laid out for me in college, the ambiguity of my future in the field was a chasm that I felt unprepared to cross. Thankfully, the intern psychologist I was seeing at the time reminded me, "We can feel one way and act in another."

One truth I have come to understand is I have always had the ability to feel one way and act another. In grad school that manifested with constantly feeling out of place but continuing to trudge through to meet my goal of becoming a Master of Social Work.

We all have unique life journeys drawing us to work in the mental health field, but that can be easy to forget when all of your colleagues seem to come from similar backgrounds, and you do not. Somewhere, along the way, my brain began to latch onto the differences between me and my cohort. Those differences included political and ideological perspectives, age, personality, and gender. I felt as if I was out to prove something, not to myself, but to the system. Looking back, I wanted desperately to belong and yet I was never sure why I cared so much in the first place.

This feeling of professional uncertainty remained after graduation even when I was brought into multiple interviews and offered various entry-level roles. Ultimately, I would accept a clinician role at a Crisis Stabilization Unit for children and adolescents (where kiddos went when placed on a psychiatric hold). I wish I could say I found acceptance of the completely natural anxiety that comes with a new position, but that's not my story. Instead, I began to feel more comfortable in my role through repetition and through fumbling through mistakes. Yet, as my comfort increased my uncertainty and anxiety about my place in the field continued to gain momentum.

At the time those around me attempted to quiet those thoughts of not fitting in by categorizing it as "Imposter Syndrome." I understood that idea and could relate to the feeling of "I don't belong here" or "I am not a good social worker" but an interaction with a 15-year-old on a psychiatric hold profoundly shifted my perspective.

The young man was placed in our care after attempting to overdose on Xanax while intoxicated by alcohol. Collateral from parents revealed a significant pattern of unsafe and impulsive behaviors. His history of aggression towards hospital staff led to difficulty finding placement. On his second day of the hold, the young man noticed my necklace... a necklace I forgot that I had on. The silver necklace was the logo of a Norwegian black metal band *Dark Funeral*. Apparently, the young man shared my affinity for the genre and almost immediately his presentation went from guarded to open. Over the next handful of days, we were able to communicate more effectively and look at plausible coping strategies and safety planning around self-harm behaviors.

Now, this scenario may seem innocuous, but it revealed to me both the problem and the solution I had been wrestling with since I started my career. I had been attempting to hide aspects of myself I had judged as not aligned with the field of social work. I was focused on the picture of a social worker painted by my experience in higher education and watching my associates, instead of who I truly was at my core.

Somewhere along the way and to my discontent, there was a split in the way I saw myself. There was the social worker version of self and the personal interpretation of self which I saw as non-helpful to my career and more importantly, non-helpful to others. That experience with the young death metal fan solidified the idea that although I bring my training, knowledge, and expertise to my role, I also need to bring with me all of what makes me who I am: the authentic self and my unique passions and interests.

Nowadays in a private practice setting, I use various tools to bring my authentic self to work: before each session, I listen to a few minutes of my favorite heavy metal artists, I wear concert t-shirts underneath my "professional" attire, and I do short breathing exercises along with a personal mantra when feeling stressed.

When not at work, I find ways to acknowledge my professional abilities and how they have positively integrated into my life. This can show up by being able to be more mindful and actively engaged with friends or family. It can also appear when I notice a new meaning to a lyric based on my understanding of the cultural impact on the writer. More often than not, I consider how my appreciation of who I am at my core allows me to better understand my clients.

Of course, these are tools unique to me, but I encourage all those in the field of mental health to identify some tools for honoring the authentic self. We are never simply professionals in this space to be judged solely by arbitrary measures like degrees and pay scales. We are always "whole-ass humans" deserving of respect and love. No matter our backgrounds. No matter our interests.

And at the end of the day, the "whole-ass humans" inside each of us can create impactful change for those around us, no matter who we are at our core.

13

FINDING HUMANNESS

WHAT MY TIME AS AN IN-PRISON COUNSELOR TAUGHT ME

MICHELLE JIO, LMFT

IN NOVEMBER OF LAST YEAR, I walked into my new job at the county jail. To most of my family and friends' chagrin, this was a job I willingly sought out because I wanted to provide psychotherapy in a custody setting. I was assigned to the highest security unit for men who were diagnosed with serious mental illness and were too assaultive to integrate with others. Because of this, they are locked in single cells for most of the day and the only time spent out of the cell is absolutely alone.

I reasoned with my loved ones that this was the most vulnerable population that had slipped through every crack of the mental health system. And in my naivete, I thought that this was the last safety net– the final frontier–where I could offer them the gift of therapy.

At this time, I was also facing a crisis in my own personal life, and I was desperately seeking validation that I was worthy and good. Looking back now, I think I gravitated to the jail in the hopes of proving that every person is redeemable no matter what they've done–that we are all deserving of love in spite of our worst mistakes. I knew that the majority of my clients had been accused of serious crimes which meant that most providers would not want to work with them. At the time, I also felt that this is where I belonged because of the shame I was feeling from my own mistakes in life; this was my version of "doing time".

When I stepped onto my assigned unit for the first time, I was left truly breathless. I was astounded by the environment. As much as I had heard l stories from others who had worked in custody settings, nothing would have prepared me for actually seeing with my own eyes forty men locked in single cells no bigger than a walk-in closet, with only a small window to look out of for almost twenty hours of the day. As I went into the pod, I heard many of the clients yelling and screaming out of their cells, most of it seems nonsensical to me, some of it hostile and threatening.

My nervous system went into overdrive and I felt myself in a state of hypervigilance, although that state is somewhat comfortable and "normal" for me. I prided myself in working in other crisis settings where I was placed into potentially dangerous situations. I'm not sure if I had to prove that I could help others in the direst of straits, or if my constant restlessness made calmer environments intolerable to me. I didn't think I would feel fear working with these men, but on the first day, I wondered if my hubris steered me down the wrong path.

My sense of shock and awe continued for several weeks, even months, as I started to sit in the same room with my clients. My clients wore wrist and leg shackles that were then chained to a desk in order for me to meet with them. This is due to their high-security status. Almost all my clients have been diagnosed with Schizophrenia Spectrum Disorders and most are severely decompensated and floridly psychotic.

I initially felt wide-eyed and completely lost in an alternate reality where I had no idea where to start and how to help. So many of these men are not even oriented to their surroundings. Instead, they are trapped in their own waking nightmares where they are persecuted by the CIA, by ghosts and aliens, by kidnappers holding them hostage, or by villainous doctors who are trying to run malicious experiments on them. All their senses scream to them that they are not safe, and therefore, they are unpredictable and sometimes volatile. Most people do not know how to respond to these men and sometimes react in invalidating ways which further confirms to the client that they are not safe.

Though my clients' presentations are far from the baseline of "normative" society, I came to find that their delusions were tangible representations of common emotions and beliefs that many, if not all of us, feel or think at one time or another. Their complicated web of delusions protects them from facing the reality of unbearable pain from past trauma, current life circumstances, and undeniable loss. Although this is an oversimplification, I strongly believe that the delusions that plague people with psychosis are the concrete illustrations of defense mechanisms we all employ to get through life.

One client had the fixed delusion that law enforcement had kidnapped him and placed him in an eternal time loop in which the same day repeats itself. The life circumstances that support his delusion are that he repeatedly gets arrested over and over again in an endless cycle. He feels a sense of stuckness, helplessness, and impotence that all of us can feel when we can't figure out how to get out of a bad situation or change our habits.

Another client suffered a severe traumatic brain injury as a teen and therefore had cognitive deficits and functional impairments as an adult. He had delusions of grandeur, such as being a CIA agent, the captain of the entire jail, or the owner of tech companies. He often yelled at deputies, asserting that they should answer to him because of his prestige. These grandiose delusions help him not face the painful incompetence he feels from the impairments; only in brief moments, would he disclose that his feelings have been hurt when people call him "stupid."

Many of the clients had delusional beliefs about their crimes that explained their actions because facing the immense shame and guilt from their mistakes would be otherwise unsurvivable. Their waking nightmares kept them safe from the truths that would be worse than their persecutory delusions.

The barriers that usually separate thoughts and feelings from sensory experiences dissolve away under the weight of psychosis. Suddenly, the fear you feel about being negatively judged by others manifests into whispers you hear through the walls, taunting you day in and day out. Or, the reasonable distrust you feel toward your environment now turns into chemical smells emanating from the food which looks tampered with and poisoned. With no solid container for intense emotions and unresolved trauma, the world starts to melt together like surrealist art.

Although I still often feel lost working in the deep tunnels and cavernous expanses of psychosis, I've seen the relief on my client's faces when I can identify the core feelings that underlie the delusions and hallucinations. Validating these emotions seems to bring about some comfort in an environment where most are repelled by these clients' behaviors. So much of the emotional content that creates the bedrock for their psychosis is highly relatable and easy to empathize with. I've started to love working with the men in my unit although there are many days I still feel bewildered, triggered by countertransference, or scared by their more dangerous reactions to their internal reality.

After months of doing this work, I still believe that everyone maintains their humanness and that is what remains deserving of love despite our worst mistakes. I remain hopeful for our ability to make amends for the harm we cause others and to heal ourselves. What I also notice is that the jail has become a metaphor for my internal world. The parts of myself that are in the most pain are isolated and exiled to the closed-off corners of my mind, typically only becoming visible in threatening or undesirable ways.

When these parts rise to the surface, I push them back behind locked doors and walls of thick metal because I'm so fearful to let them out. They have to be constrained by some invisible shackles before I feel safe enough to work with them, but at the end of the day, they need my care and attention. We *all* need care and attention. All of our pieces, all of our parts are worthy of someone sitting down with them, and letting them know that they are seen, and they are safe.

14

FEELS LIKE COMING HOME

KELLY DUNN, LMFT

THE FIRST THING I noticed when Olivia* walked into my office for our first session was the look of fear and sadness in her eyes. She immediately sat down and started to weep. Through her tears and runny nose, she shared a feeling of pain and emptiness inside of her. It was a feeling of uncertainty and confusion about herself, her emotions, and her life circumstances. She shared about her contentious relationship with her mother and her struggles with money, resulting in a need to move back in with her mother and stepfather.

Toward the end of the session, she looked at me with a pleading look in her eyes, asking me if she would ever feel okay again. She asked me if I knew of others who were struggling with this much sadness and who came to feel better. While I know as a therapist that I can't promise anything, I do know that I can give hope to those who are suffering. At that moment, I reassured her that, yes, I had seen people make dramatic, positive changes in their lives through therapy. But they needed to be open to experiencing all that life had to offer: the good feelings along with the bad.

Olivia described her emotional pain as a "pit" in her stomach and an ache from uncertainty about who she was. In talking with her over time, there was a realization between the two of us that this pain stemmed from her complete lack of confidence in who she was, and in *understanding* who she was. She felt she didn't know herself. That thought alone was enough to bring tears to her eyes.

When a person feels this way, it isn't easy to answer the question, "Who am I?" or "What do I care about?" or "What are my interests?" This identity crisis stems from a lifetime of needing to care about *other* people's needs/wants/interests/rules. Olivia and I talked about patterns of relationships in her life and ways that she abandoned her own needs and internal cues.

Over the weeks that followed, Olivia and I talked about how to notice feelings and sensations in her body. We talked about noticing her body's response to everything she did in her life – driving, walking, playing with her dog, being in the presence of others, and reading a book. She began to prioritize herself by noticing these things and giving her own body the attention it had never received.

Olivia began to sense a feeling of calm in her body when she focused on her feelings at the moment. She began to notice feelings of ease in her body with calming music and feelings of excitement when she got home from work to see her dog. Slowly, she began to ask herself questions that were becoming easier to answer, like "What are my interests?" What do I want" and "Who am I?" With intentional reflection, these questions no longer felt depleting, but rewarding. They felt like coming home.

Olivia isn't my only client that has experienced deep uncertainty about who they currently are, and who they are becoming. The process of coming into oneself takes a lot of different forms. They may sound like:

"I feel like I have to prove something to myself"

"Sometimes I wonder what the point is."

"I have confidence in myself, I know I can do it."

"I'm just so fed up."

"Sometimes I wonder who I am."

"I feel invisible in my family."

"I have something to look forward to and that feels good."

"I think we have three purposes: survival, to think, and to feel."

"I wish I could control my understanding of who I am."

I have learned that this process is not about finding an answer. It is about listening, really listening, and not simply hearing to respond. My job is to provide a space that acknowledges their experience and strengthens the inner voice that says, "You are right to feel this way, of *course*, you feel this way."

For those like Olivia, practicing self-love allows an individual to understand who they truly are, and what they want, need, and desire. We practice imagining someone else who appears to have self-love. Do we wonder what it feels like in their body? Their *whole* body. How does self-love feel in your feet? Your legs? Your stomach? Your arms? Your neck? Your head? Then, we practice imagining what self-love looks like in actions. How would life be different, what would we *do* differently if we incorporated self-love into every one of our actions? Herein lies our true identity.

To lose oneself, one's understanding of "*Who I am*" is one of the greatest pains in life. It is a shell of an existence. And yet, we don't often see that this is where the pain lies. It doesn't lie in a bad relationship, it doesn't lie in behaviors we wish we could change, it doesn't lie in the job we hate. It lies in a loss of self, a loss of knowledge, and really understanding that we are worthy.

To feel whole again, we must bring back this knowledge. This part of ourselves got lost a long time ago and has learned to reside in the dark crevices of our being. But it is possible to shine our light here once again, Olivia is living proof.

This is how we return to feeling at home in our bodies, and the definition of confidence, we feel at peace no matter where we are and no matter what is going on outside. It is to know, on a visceral level, that we are worthy, and we are home.

1

---

1. *Name has been changed to protect privacy.*

15

PLANTING SEEDS
THOUGHTS ON TRUSTING THE PROCESS

ADRIANA AUCOIN-UNRUHE, LMFT

GROWING UP, I never imagined myself as a therapist. In fact, as a teen, I dreamed of attending art school. But I struggled with self-doubt and worried that I would never be able to make it as an artist, so I decided to be more "practical" and choose a different career path that I hoped would come with a little more certainty to it. Little did I know that regardless of the career path I chose, uncertainty in myself and my role would be something I would have to continue to work to overcome.

As a freshman in college, I found myself fascinated by psychology and thought that choosing this as a career field might also be a way to help make a difference in people's lives, even if it was just a small difference. I did not yet have the self-awareness or confidence in myself to know that by making this choice I was starting my journey of helping others heal and learn more about themselves, while I grew right alongside them.

No Stranger to Therapy

The idea of attending therapy was not a new concept to me. I had lost my father to cancer as a child and found myself lost after his death. I was angry and sad, and it felt like no one else would be able to understand what I was going through. I struggled with anxiety about losing someone else who was close to me, and yet I also pushed my friends away and isolated myself from them. I remember seeing a counselor at school at that young age and how much of a difference that made for me to be able to have a space to go and talk, or to just be. I still remember the photo of my father that I brought to my counseling session one day to make a tribute for him, and how I decorated the frame by gluing down different buttons all around the photo. They were purple buttons, his favorite color.

Around that same time, I also did sand tray therapy. I remember how much I looked forward to getting to select different figurines out of the therapist's cabinet and "play" in the sand, and how much I enjoyed getting to create new little worlds each week within the containment of that space. Little did I know at the time how "playing" in the sand was also helping me work through my loss, and begin my healing process.

Later on in my childhood, after my mother started dating again, I began to feel angry, alone, and resentful. My mother and I eventually went to see a family therapist together, and this helped me express myself to her with the support of another grown-up. Although the therapist was someone neutral, it also felt like they really cared about me and wanted to help. I finally felt like I was able to be heard by my mother. Conversely, with the help of this therapist, she was able to understand my perspective.

Through the ups and downs of childhood, I continued to navigate struggles and feelings of loneliness with the help of caring therapists. Some may find it surprising that I had never considered therapy as a career path since I had been able to benefit from it myself as a child. Little did I know at the time that during those experiences with therapy as a young person, I was beginning to plant the seeds to become the therapist I am today. I now recognize that those experiences have helped me to better understand what some of my clients may be going through and be able to support them during their own journey.

The Onset of Imposter Syndrome

Fast forward to my early twenties, when I had just graduated college and gone through a brutal break-up and was feeling lost yet again. I returned to old patterns of childhood and adolescence, trying to find comfort by escaping into self-destructive ways. Around this same time, I also started working full-time in the mental health field, a dynamic time to say the least!

A few years later, I took a leap of faith and decided to apply for graduate school to pursue a career as a therapist. I remember being shocked that I got accepted into the graduate program and questioning myself once again: "*Had they made a mistake in accepting me into this program? Did I have what it takes to be a therapist? After all, I didn't even really have my own life figured out just yet! How could I possibly help other people?*"

On that first day of graduate school, I recall feeling like I didn't really belong there. I was worried that I hadn't made the right choice and questioned if I would ever be "good enough" to be a therapist one day. In my mind, I believed my classmates must have had something that I didn't, that their life was all figured out while I still worked to navigate my own challenges.

However, as the weeks went by, I started to feel more comfortable. I began to realize that my classmates and I were all in the same position -- no one in my cohort really knew what they were doing, not yet anyways. We were all learning together. No matter our past, each one of us was a beginner, starting from a place of not knowing.

Although my classmates and I were different ages, from different cultural and socioeconomic backgrounds, and with very different life experiences, we were all there to learn and grow as future therapists. Over time, I realized that comparing myself to others and believing that they had something I didn't was just my own self-doubt and inner criticism being projected onto others.

Becoming a therapist didn't mean I already had it all together. It simply meant that I was in the process of figuring things out and making a commitment to continuing my own personal and professional growth.

Planting Seeds

My time in graduate school has taught me that sometimes we just have to fake it until we make it. Sometimes, life requires us to keep showing up and pushing ourselves to be vulnerable and to try something new, even when it feels scary and takes a lot of courage to do so. By coming from a place of being humble, embracing the not knowing, and being willing to let our guard down, we can gradually be sculpted by the experience and grow into a new version of ourselves. This was the mindset I had to develop over time to help me get through graduate school. I had to learn to give myself grace, accept my imperfections, and embrace each challenge as an opportunity for growth. I now recognize this was also a part of my own healing journey, and it has helped me to become a truer and more confident version of myself.

I still remember the days leading up to providing my first therapy sessions as a trainee and having another surge of self-doubt. The usual questions came up again: *"Did I really have what it takes? Would I be good enough? Would I be able to apply what I had learned in school? Would I be able to support individuals who were going through some of the biggest challenges of their life, just as I had been helped as a child?"*

There was one day my first supervisor talked about how therapy can be like "planting seeds," and this concept has been something that has really stuck with me over the years. Sometimes, a client isn't ready to do the work yet, or the circumstances and timing aren't quite right for them to be able to make changes in their lives. I reflected on my journey, and this resonated with my own experiences in therapy as a child. Although I hadn't seen a dramatic improvement from each therapy session I attended, they were helping to plant the seeds that were needed for the deeper healing that would come later, when I was ready.

Sometimes, we aren't going to see the progress that we have helped a client make, but that doesn't mean we haven't made an impact. Each time we show up for our clients, present our genuine selves and give our best, we are helping to create growth and providing a reparative experience for them. This may be the first time in the client's life that they have a relationship that feels safe and predictable. The end of the therapeutic relationship may be the first time that the client can have a healthy goodbye. By just showing up and being there each week, we may have helped to plant a seed that will continue to be nurtured and grow over time. Even though we might not be around to watch that seed eventually sprout, that doesn't mean we weren't a part of that growth.

I still struggle to this day, even as a licensed therapist, with questioning whether I am good enough or whether I have what it takes. When I consider a new career opportunity or taking on something new that is outside of my comfort zone, that little voice of self-doubt still comes up: *"Is there someone else who would do a better job? Is there someone else who has more experience? Do I have what it takes to do this?"*

But then I remind myself of those seeds I have helped to plant, that I do have things to offer, and that everyone has to start with no experience at some point. Every therapist has to go through their first therapy session with a client. Every supervisor has to go through having their first supervisee. By getting caught up in the cycle of questioning whether we are good enough, or whether we have what it takes, we are holding ourselves back from the chance to grow as individuals. Part of the beauty of working in this field is that there is always something new you can learn and that each day can bring new experiences.

Finding My Voice and Trusting the Process

It has been about ten years now since the first day of my graduate school journey. Although I still struggle with that voice of self-doubt from time to time, it is starting to become quieter now, and I am finding myself coming into my own and beginning to trust that I have what it takes. I now know that sometimes admitting that we don't have all the answers, and acknowledging that we are human and we make mistakes, is what can help us continue to grow and become better therapists. I am by no means perfect. I have had my own challenges that I am continuing to work through and heal from, but I now know with confidence that I am enough and I have helped make a difference for my clients.

One of the graduate professors who has had an impact on my journey used another phrase that I often come back to when navigating the therapeutic relationship: "trusting the process." To me, trusting the process means that we have to give in to that uncomfortable feeling, give in to the not knowing, trust that we do have what it takes, and have faith that it will all work out the way it is supposed to.

During times of self-doubt, I remind myself of this concept. Even though there are some days when I may still feel like I don't know what I am doing, that I am not good enough, or that I should have done something differently, I remind myself that there are many other people, and many other therapists, who have felt this same way.

We all have to start as beginners and move from a place of not knowing, to one of experience and understanding. We have to give our own seeds time to be nurtured, trust in the process, and believe that in time something beautiful will grow from those seeds. Being a great therapist doesn't mean you have it all together, or that self-doubt never trickles in. It means that you are willing to show up and become better, day after day, and know that your clients are better for it, and trust that growth happens, even when we may not see it.

16

UNSTOPPABLE

GABRIELLE MCQUEEN, MS, MA, AMFT

I DEVELOPED the mentality of being unstoppable at a very young age. When I was 13, on a cold December morning, I woke up to find my mother lifeless on our living room couch. My mother had suffered from a heart attack in her sleep. There I was, an only child that was suddenly an orphan and ward of the court.

My biological father was known but loved from a distance. I recall meeting him once, in person, at a custody hearing shortly after my mother's passing. I was happy to see him, but he was not the family I was meant to live with. Because of this, immediately following my mother's passing, I relocated from Oakland, California where I had lived with my mom to Union City California where I would live with my uncle and aunt.

The transition to moving into their home was smoother than many may expect but I was used to staying at their home for long periods due to my mother being sick throughout most of my childhood. My uncle was more of a father figure than just an uncle and he was my mother's older brother and closest sibling. I believe some of my mother's witty personality and sass came from her experiences growing up with three older brothers.

If you're someone that's into horoscopes, then you would immediately recognize that my mother was a true Virgo. If making things happen with grace was a person, then it would be her. She was loved and respected by many and had an aura that attracted others to seek support from her. Understandably, my mother was an amazing counselor and case manager. So much so that her entire caseload, colleagues, and classmates attended her funeral and all had many positive memories to share.

At the time of her passing, my mother was at the tail end of her second year of graduate school at Holy Names University studying to receive her Master's in Counseling. I always admired my mother's drive and determination. She finished anything she started and never accepted "no" as a final answer. She was, without a doubt, unstoppable in her love and commitment to helping others. It's only fitting that I followed my mother's footsteps, not only being a Virgo at the core but also in achieving nearly every goal I've set for myself.

To this day, I give all thanks to my mother for being honest with me throughout my childhood regarding her physical health and thanks to God for helping guide me through the grief of losing my mother. Since she was a single mother, I often witnessed her very ill in the emergency room as she waited in agonizing pain. My mother was terrified of needles and I recall holding back tears while softly asking the nurses "Please don't hurt my mom" while holding her hand and caressing her back while they input her IV amongst other anesthesia. That's a lot for a child to witness.

While waiting for my uncle to pick me up from the emergency room, I would often find myself imagining I was somewhere other than the hospital to help cope with the flood of emotions I felt at that moment. My mother would tell me not to be afraid and to always trust in God's timing and purpose and to know that although she may not see me graduate from college; she would always be with me. That I was unstoppable and could do anything I set my mind to.

Unfortunately, my mother wasn't able to witness me graduate from the eighth grade because she passed 6 months before my graduation. As heartbreaking as this moment was, I carried her unbreakable spirit as I continued to navigate the world before me.

In the months after my mother's death, I recall feeling like I was stuck in a dream that I would never be able to awake from; a sense of cold and emptiness filled my body and created a home of protection. The idea that kept propelling me forward was that I had to make my mother proud. From that day forward, I was determined to be successful in life and to make sure I left behind a legacy that my mother would admire. Little did I know that the title of "unstoppable" would lead me forward in my future career.

Fast forward 16 years in the future from that fateful moment when I was thirteen years old. As a new graduate student at a very prestigious university, I was eager to get my feet wet in the world of mental health and decided to apply to my first position as a Therapeutic Behavioral Counselor with a local non-profit agency in Northern California. A flood of emotions rushed through my body and mind as I submitted my application in hopes of being a selected candidate and fulfilling my mother's legacy as a therapist for at-risk youth and families.

I recalled participating in company picnics, school graduations, and youth retreats with my mother and her company during my early childhood and adolescent years. I admired my mother's service as a case manager within our community. She showed unconditional love and respect to everyone she met. Regardless of their socioeconomic status or background; my mother would take her clients in as if they were a member of our family. There were many times when I felt jealous (classic only child syndrome) when my mother would bring along one of her teen clients to one of our weekend outings to a museum or screenplay. But now, I understand this was part of her big heart.

My mother wanted to show at-risk youth that they can be a product of their environment and still be successful in life. She exposed her clients to many experiences that they may not have ever been able to be a part of. She encouraged her clients to maintain good grades while guiding them in applying for scholarship programs and local enrichment camps which they were able to attend for free just based on maintaining satisfactory grades.

After watching the joy my mother instilled in others without a thought of what she could receive in return; I knew I wanted to do the same for others. Unbeknownst to me, I was embarking on a ride of a lifetime that would be rewarding and yet challenging to its core. Just as my mother had been before me, I was paving the way to make our world a better place, and along with that came plenty of heartache.

At age 26, entering into my second year of a 3.5 year graduate program, I was selected as a new hire and began my first week of work as a Therapeutic Behavioral Coach while full-time in a Master of Counseling graduate program. I was carrying three classes per week and working forty hours; I was hustling. Hustling has always been my baseline, it's my go-to mode. This part of me is a blessing and a curse because if you're someone who doesn't have a strong sense of personal boundaries, then you can quickly burn out. I was so eager to learn and admired the seasoned therapists at the agency; I just wanted to support people of color and inner-city youth to show others that nothing is impossible in life.

I received my first caseload as a TBS Coach and Clinical Supervisor soon after I began my new job at the time as the director of the mental health department at the non-profit agency. I'll call this particular woman "Cruella." I've given her this name because although she was fashionable and dressed like a businesswoman on Wall Street; she was ruthless and cold just like the character from *101 Dalmatians*.

Whenever she walked into the office, everyone became sheepish and fearful to ask for her help in anything due to being afraid of the condescending, critical feedback she would eagerly give out. Honestly, If Meryl Streep in *The Devil Wears Prada* and Cruella had a baby then I'd imagine this supervisor would be their protege. At my first interaction, I honestly admired her fashion sense, her self-confidence, and her consistent work ethic. I looked up to this woman. I did not care that she proudly exuded white privilege in the workplace and that she was disliked by nearly everyone at the agency; I was determined to form my own professional relationship with Cruella.

As the months passed on, I began to notice Cruella's true personality which was not friendly, welcoming, motivational, supportive, or consistent. Instead, I experienced multiple rude emails, microaggressions, and micro-managing for nearly four years during my employment with the agency. I remember once asking Cruella for support on a case and her response was along the lines of "Why is this so complicated for you? I am wondering if you are even fit for this position since you seem to be unable to utilize the common sense and basic skills of a therapist."

I rushed to my car and cried hysterically while on the phone with my boyfriend at the time. I felt so defeated; crushed and began to experience thoughts of self-hate, and pessimism and doubted every decision I made for months following that email encounter. This behavior of low self-esteem continued for nearly a year after receiving that email as well as multiple forms of systemic racism brought on by Cruella and the upper management. For all my mother had taught me, that I was strong, capable, and confident, Cruella's words and demeanor seemed to be stripping me of.

As I continued to keep my head above water in this toxic situation, my PTO was declined two days before I planned to leave for my trip after asking multiple times when it would be approved or denied. Cruella's response was along these lines: that my productivity was low that month and I would need to meet my productivity before she approved any of my PTO.

I had no idea that she was skating on thin ice regarding employee rights and other things as I tried to keep my head down and play by these rules. I began to converse with my colleagues about multiple issues I ran into with Cruella to see if others who were non-black were experiencing similar situations and to my surprise, they were not. Once I discovered that other employees did not experience this same workplace harassment and systemic racism, I asked myself a question that regularly came to mind in the years since my mother's passing: how would mom handle this?

I wanted to make her feel every bit of discomfort she imposed on me during my time with the agency. I wanted to cry, scream, and call her every name in the book. Yet, my mother's warm aura came to me once again and I thought "I'm going to professionally kill her with kindness."

After sitting in my car and crying for what felt like an hour after understanding that I was being singled out for this mistreatment, I walked back upstairs and began documenting everything she had said to me that was unethical and along the lines of workplace harassment. I recall as soon as I walked in the door after an emotional lunch hour, Cruella rolled her eyes and said "Hmmm, took a long lunch, huh?" with a smirk on her face.

I smiled back, whipped my hair, and replied "Absolutely, because my mental health is more important than pleasing people and last I checked, we're given an hour lunch but thanks for checking on me." I walked away feeling irritated but oddly proud that I spoke up for myself, unlike other employees who probably would have apologized for taking their lunch.

From that interaction, I no longer felt inferior to Cruella. It was like my mom stepped into me and said "Not today, Cruella!" I was no longer afraid of her. I walked into the office with my head high and heels higher to the point that Cruella started to make snarky comments about my attire and once told me that I'm too curvy to wear dresses to work. I made sure to note that comment in my binder of things to report once I was ready. I would walk into the office every day and make it a point to tap on her door and say "good morning" with a smile and confident walk back to my desk.

I stayed ahead of the curve by making sure I met all deadlines and was on time for every meeting. I could tell it bothered her because she then started to be passive-aggressive and struggled with my hard boundaries. She would intentionally send me emails and texts late at night and during the weekends. Since we only worked Monday through Friday 9-5, I only responded to such emails and texts during my working hours. Cruella would give me attitude and I would politely remind her that "Fortunately, I do not work on the weekends or past 5 pm." I was unstoppable.

After the appropriate amount of time had passed and I had gathered my evidence, I eventually went to the human resources office and made a formal complaint against Cruella. Unfortunately, I was let go and three months later they mailed me a severance package. I assume they did this because they became aware of the potential lawsuit they could have faced if I chose to take that route. Six months after I was let go, I heard from former colleagues that Cruella was also fired due to harassment claims and engaging in unethical behavior that was against the company's policies. Instead of relief, I felt betrayed. I felt like I was the scapegoat and no one believed me until Cruella was fired.

Before the harassment claims, the feedback I received from colleagues was to just "stick it out." My mother would have rolled over in her grave if she knew I was allowing someone like Cruella to steal my joy and I knew "sticking it out" was just not me. I felt like I had a higher calling in life. I always told myself that God did not bring me all this way to be miserable and unhappy. So I pushed on to bigger opportunities and didn't let my experience with Cruella tarnish my self-motivation to be a successful therapist.

Less than a month after being let go from the non-profit agency, I was hired as a Therapeutic Behavioral Clinician with a larger non-profit agency within Santa Clara County. This new assignment immediately felt refreshing. I enjoyed the two-week training experience at their headquarters and loved my team and coworkers in the many other departments within the agency. For once in my life, I felt safe at work and appreciated. My supervisor at the time was a few years younger than me, but she is still to this day one of the most supportive supervisors I've had and we have become really good friends over the years.

During my time with the agency, I often felt my mother's presence when supporting individuals and families within the inner-city limits and especially in East San Jose. I experienced so much growth, both professionally and personally. While at this agency, I noticed I was ready to accept all things meant for me. I got engaged to my high school sweetheart, moved into our first high-rise apartment, and was introduced to the owner of a private practice in Campbell, California. I've always wanted to own a private practice and was excited to be allowed to join an amazing group practice located in Campbell.

I was confident the moment I met Amanda, the practice owner, that I would fit right in and would grow so much with her company. Little did I know, Amanda would end up becoming a friend, supervisor, and mentor all in one. Amanda, allowed me to be myself and encourage my entrepreneurship every step of the way. She's been a cheerleader in my corner since the moment I met her.

After being with Yes to Therapy for 4 years, I noticed the growth in the company and felt confident in taking the next step in my career. Again, I could hear my mother's voice in my ear saying "Go get it!, YOU GOT THIS!" So, I went after my dream and launched my group telehealth private practice, Open Minds Marriage, and Family Counseling Services Corp.

My mother and uncle always taught me to network and remain friends with the "right" people. I realized I was becoming burnt out from one on one therapy and direct services and was looking for a way out while still making a comfortable living. I remained friends with many therapists from the agency Cruella had worked at and reached out to them about joining my practice. I hired them on the spot.

Before I knew it, I had four employees and my own practice. Compare this to a young woman who was chastised for taking a lunch break and denied PTO. As the young kids say, I was "shook." The more I leaned into my own joy, happiness, and confidence, the more unstoppable I became.

A part of me would have never thought I would have achieved this lifelong goal of mine at such a young age. I'm now 35, married, and a new mom to a highly active two-year-old boy. I often reflect on my childhood and begin to cry because I recognize that I've overcome so much in such a short amount of time. I pour love and self-confidence into my son every chance I can and cherish every moment because I know far too well how short life is.

My mother passed away when she was only 43 years old. She physically missed so much of my life and I know in many ways that I have made her very proud. I hope to continue to motivate other therapists on their journey and all black women to go after everything they want in life and nothing is too big to achieve. My uncle always told me to think of at least five business ideas per day and to write them down. I truly believe this life hack has helped me achieve many things in my life journey. This is my story and it's just the beginning, I know I have so much more to achieve. I'm here for a short time, not a long time, and like Gen Z says "let's keep it lit." With my mother's light glowing bright inside of me, I will continue to be *unstoppable*.

17

THERAPY IS MY "WHY"

ANONYMOUS AUTHOR

OVERALL, I had the ideal childhood. I grew up as the youngest of three daughters from two extraordinarily loving parents in the East San Francisco Bay Area, otherwise known as suburbia. My father is a third-generation plumber and my mom was a "stay-at-home mom." Despite my father being alcohol-free since '83, our family and extended family were dysfunctionally alcoholic.

To add to the complexity of growing up in an alcoholic household, I found myself with undiagnosed ADHD with severe anxiety. Because of this, I was required to have unique behavioral plans with every teacher, all the way through Kindergarten to grade five. It was how these teachers thought I could more effectively learn, but it caused even more anxiety in the school setting. I dreaded student-teacher conferences. Though I had "behavioral plans" in each class, I felt that I had no support in school and was told to "figure it out" by teachers when something didn't make sense, or that I was "crazy," when I voiced my discomfort.

I learned to shove most of my problems under the rug by giving my best effort like everyone else, even though my learning problems and home life were having an effect on school experience. Then, therapy entered my world, and everything changed.

By the time I started middle school, my parent's attention became focused on my middle sister's attitude, struggling grades, and partying, instead of the struggles I was facing at school. In the classroom, things weren't much better. Instead of behavioral plans for my distracting "class clown" comments, my middle school teachers would kick me out of the classroom. I can remember sitting outside of my sixth-grade English class, watching the rain, and thinking for the first time that the world might be a better place without me.

My first exposure to therapy was as a young child hearing my mom speak about the legendary therapist named Tom, who saved my grandparents' lives and worked magic in my parent's relationship. Despite my excessive energy and attention issues, I managed to keep decent grades. In fact, I forced myself to excel and keep up with the challenging academic and athletic environment of the Bay Area suburbs. I learned that I could use my excess energy to my advantage in sports and that I could fool others, including myself at times, by feigning external happiness.

By middle school, I was ahead in classes and playing sports year-round. I begged and pleaded with my mother, explaining that my sister was the problem and "I am handling everything fine so why therapy?" My mom explained to me that she wanted an outlet for me

It turns out that lying to your therapist about being happy is not only a waste of money but creates other problems, too. The first time I drank while living in my freshman college dorms, I wondered why I had not tried drinking sooner. It was an instant relief for the zillions of thoughts constantly going through my mind. It also inflated my self-esteem which had been crippled since elementary school parent-teacher conferences. It also allowed me to put off all of my problems with the mindset "Oh, I will figure it out tomorrow." However, as many of those who struggle with addiction know all too well, tomorrow did not come for about another decade. Alcohol brought instant relief for me than my psychiatric medication for anxiety and depression.

Towards the end of the decade, I was hired to do community relations and marketing with an inpatient hospital where I learned a lot about codependency and co-occurring disorders. I was also visiting a payday loan office every other week to make it to my next paycheck, praying that each visit would be my last. I went through rock bottom after rock bottom, feeling sick and tired of feeling sick and tired.

On February 6, 2020, I felt like I was hallucinating about the substances I took the evening my partner told me they did not love me anymore. At this moment, I had an epiphany. The epiphany was the blessing of desperation to turn my life around. I realized: "How could someone love me if I could not love myself first? I do not want to go through *another* break up self medicating with drugs" I had spent a decade taking care of everyone else but myself. I made the heartbreaking and necessary decision to move home, thinking I may never see my puppy and partner ever again.

When most of the world was hitting 'rock bottom' during the COVID-19 pandemic, it was a period of immensely beautiful spiritual expansion for me. Although I was furloughed by the end of the first month of the pandemic, I had the privilege to spend the majority of my days stand-up paddle boarding (believe it or not) in Vallejo, California, and being of service to my family.

By October 2020, my partner, our dog, and I reconnected after nine months apart through our love for music. I found myself gaining momentum in therapy and recovery both personally and professionally.

 All things mental health, including honesty in therapy, became my why.

Dedicated to Grandmother who was one of my first "clients." She passed away on 2/26/17, at 2:26 pm — By coincidence, I have been in recovery since 2/6/20.

18

NEVER TOO LATE

LORI YOUNG, GRADUATE STUDENT

I WAS A 53-YEAR-OLD WOMAN, wife of 31 years, mom of 2 adult sons, and grandmother who decided to pursue the dream of completing graduate school, uncovering my passion, and discovering the real me. When I was in my late 40s and my sons were moving towards independence, I started to panic. This was a scary time for me because I was starting to realize that I didn't know who or what I was besides a wife and a mom. But with the patience and support of a wonderful therapist, I was able to put one foot in front of another and began to uncover who I was at my core.

I remember trying to figure out how to write a personal essay that would make me stand out and appear unique to whoever was reading these in the Marriage and Family Therapy graduate application process. I decided to write about how I have experienced trauma, abandonment, feelings of fight or flight, and watching the effects of addictions and personality disorders on a family unit. I wrote about the blended family and how lucky I was to live with awesome step-parents and step-grandparents. I realized that my life experience could be helpful to others. But I never fully realized just how valuable I could be in this role until I realized there were parts that were ready to grow and change.

I came into this program with the main purpose of earning a degree in a field that dealt with a totally different population of humans than I have worked with. I was excited to work with women going through transitions and eager to change the demographic I had usually worked with: children. My whole adult life revolved around children. I was a mom, a licensed family daycare provider, and a jump rope coach. When I learned that my job would require me to work with children and their families, I was disappointed. I believed it was time for new horizons and new opportunities! I thought I had already learned I had to learn about children, and already gave all I could to the young people of today. But I soon realized it was time for me to give in a different capacity.

This change caused me to go into the second and third years of my graduate program kicking, screaming, and fighting within myself because I realized that even in my fifties, there was still so much for me to learn! I have been challenged when I thought I would not be. Not only did I have learned to relax about schoolwork and learn that children were very much a part of many mental health workers' clientele, but it was also necessary that I take the time to review my life and my choices. I have forgiven myself for waiting until I was in my fifties to go back to school and get a degree. I have been reaccessing and reevaluating what my life is going to look like with a professional career. But now it was time for me to embrace what this career was giving me and put my heart and soul into the work.

I started the second year of graduate school not even recognizing myself. I felt like a fish out of water trying just to survive. Once confident in my abilities and in life, at age fifty-three, I began to rebuild my identity and how I defined myself. It wasn't a comfortable process, but it was necessary to discover the full capacity of who I was. I keep reminding myself and will tell everyone reading this, to stay the course with integrity while staying true to *you*. I was told that I would never forget my first client and I truly believe that statement. I have a little client who is keeping me "real". So far, he has given me the greatest gift, he has taught me that I am good enough to do this work, the kind of work that I want to do while keeping a part of "me" intact.

This journey to licensure at this time in my life is not easy, but the beginning of something holistic and helpful. This year has taught me patience, and that perfection is not required! I am changing and transforming, and I look forward to this learning process that will take me to where I need and want to be in life: death of the old and rebirth of a new soul alignment, no matter the age!

Through this grad school journey, I have struggled with how to incorporate mySELF into a box that I felt professors and MFT supervisors were building for me. How would I include holistic parts of mySELF (my Reiki master skills, IFS, shamanism, somatic therapy, etc.) and the part of traditional MFT interventions? I didn't even know how to define ME, until today! I am a "humanistic family systems therapist" and I couldn't be more proud of who I will continue to become.

19

RESTORATION

JAMES GERI, LMFT

"Restoration" is a poem I wrote at a time when I was starting to gain momentum in graduate school as I pursued my goal of becoming a therapist. It was written during a dynamic time of my life: while I had gotten out of the military years before, I was still in the process of adjusting to civilian life while simultaneously pursuing an advanced degree. I was constantly learning, growing, and expanding, and after navigating several challenges, I finally learned how to embrace the unknown with open arms.

It was at this time that I started to believe that my dreams were within reach and I was beginning to remember that I was capable of achieving great things. It took a lot of blood, sweat, and tears to get where I wanted to be, and I was struck with the realization that these struggles came with a purpose, and I was ready and willing to embrace past challenges and go wherever this new part of life took me.

You will also notice that this poem is written to represent the shape of a wing. This further symbolizes the emotion I was feeling at this time: confidence that I would be able to rise from a place of newness, change, and challenges, and take flight by fully embracing what this chapter of life was offering.

Restoration

Rising o'er the distant plains
Soaring flight, the choice I make
Finally I shed these heavy chains
Last thing I'll do is hit the brake

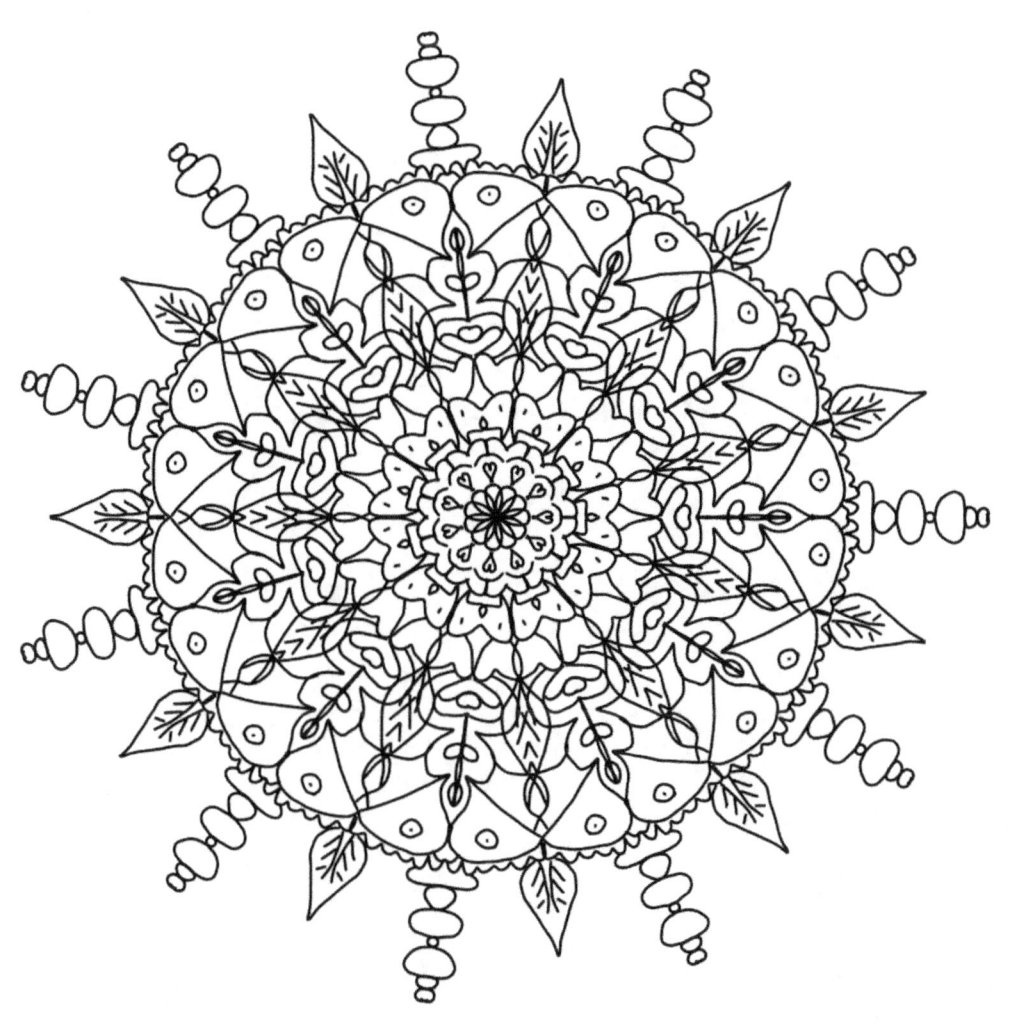

YES TO THERAPY

If you like what you have read in this book, please feel free to visit our website at www.yestotherapy.com. You can read more about Yes To Therapy, our company culture, practices, read our blogs and even purchase our **daily series!**

Our daily series is an email subscription of prompts that have an emphasis on self-esteem and confidence, all thoroughly created by our therapists at YTT.

If you would like to contact us, feel free to reach us at **info@ yestotherapy.com**